Sewing Fun Stuff!
SOFT SCULPTURE SHORTCUTS

Sewing Fun Stuff!
Soft Sculpture Shortcuts

by Lynne Farris

Illustrations by Barbara Abrelat

Sterling Publishing Co., Inc.
New York
A STERLING/SEWING INFORMATION RESOURCES BOOK

Sewing Information Resources

Owner: JoAnn Pugh-Gannon
Photography: Greg Poteet, Atlanta, Georgia
Illustration: Barbara Abrelat, Atlanta, Georgia

Book design, and production provided by Jennings & Keefe, Corte Madera, Ca.
Publishing Director: Jack Jennings
Project Manager: Janet Andrews
Electronic Page Layout: JoLynn Taylor

Library of Congress Cataloging-in-Publication Data Available

A Sterling/Sewing Information Resources Book

2 4 6 8 10 9 7 5 3 1

Published by Sterling Publishing Company, Inc.
387 Park Avenue South, New York, N.Y. 10016
Produced by Sewing Information Resources
P.O. Box 330, Wasco, Il. 60183
©1996 by Lynne Farris Designs
Distributed in Canada by Sterling Publishing
c/o Canadian Manda Group, One Atlantic Avenue, Suite 105
Toronto, Ontario, Canada, M6K 3E7
Distributed in Great Britian and Europe by Cassell PLC
Wellington House, 125 Strand, London WC2R 0BB, England
Distributed in Australia by Capricorn Link (Australia) Pty Ltd.
P.O. Box 6651, Baulkham Hills, Business Centre, NSW 2153, Australia
Printed in Hong Kong
All rights reserved

Sterling ISBN 0-8069-6164-3

4

Acknowledgements

Writing a book is never a solitary activity. This one, however, has truly become a global project as I have somehow managed to involve just about everyone I know in bringing this project to completion. Those who must be named are:

Nonie Sutton and her late husband Ben, who introduced me to the wonderful world of Bernina and pointed me toward the door at which this opportunity knocked.

Bernina of America and Fritz Gegauf AG for supporting my work and providing numerous creative opportunities for me.

April Fields for challenging me to undertake this project and encouraging me throughout the process.

Mary Asgari, my loyal friend and assistant, whose enthusiasm, creativity, tenacity, and nimble fingers have brought all of these projects to fruition.

JoAnn Pugh-Gannon, my editor, for her vision, faith, and pull-it-together encouragement.

Barbara Aberlat, talented designer, artist and writer, for her skillful illustrations which seem plucked from my mind to her pen. Truly her pictures are worth a thousand words and her patience is limitless.

Greg Poteet for his breathtaking photography.

My friend Susan Cook, whose intuitive intelligence, skillful determination, and cheerful collaboration magically transformed thousands of bits of information into this manuscript.

Jo Lynn Taylor for transforming my manuscript into a beautiful book.

Jack and Julie Pierce of Atlanta Sewing Center for support and encouragement and for keeping my machines running in tip top condition.

My brother Roland "Henry" Stubblefield, and my dear friend Lambert Greene, who have nurtured and encouraged my creative pursuits throughout my career, and who dragged me kicking and screaming into the world of computers, providing countless hours of online and on-site technical and emotional support.

My late grandmother, Adele McBurney Stubblefield, who patiently and lovingly taught me to sew.

Dedication

This book and all of my creative activities are dedicated to my mother, Kennie Lee Stafford Stubblefield, and my late father, Eben McBurney Stubblefield, whose love of beauty, creative spirits and unconditional support have inspired and sustained me throughout my life.

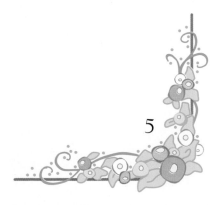

Table of Contents

Introduction 8
Chapter 1 10
  The Origins of Soft Sculpture
Chapter 2 16
  Tools and Materials
Chapter 3 26
  Sewing Machine Features and Accessories
Chapter 4 32
  How to Work with Patterns
Chapter 5 36
  Shortcuts and Specialized Sewing
  Techniques
Chapter 6 44
  Finishing Touches
Chapter 7 50
  Beginner Projects
Chapter 8 66
  Intermediate Projects
Chapter 9 92
  Advanced Projects
Chapter 10 126
  Designing Your Own Projects
Resource Guide 140
Pattern Section 141
About the Author 157
Index 158

Introduction

My fascination with soft sculpture began about fifteen years ago when I was working as an art teacher and was asked to make puppets for a school musical. Undaunted by my total lack of knowledge, I dashed to my sewing machine and began snipping, stitching and stuffing. Unencumbered by preconceived notions, I allowed my creativity and sewing skills to take over. What an exhilarating experience! Seeing those first little puppets come to life on the stage set in motion a series of events which developed into a fulfilling career as a puppetmaker, toy designer, creator of costumed characters, and textile artist.

As I began working on a wide assortment of projects with varying requirements, I was fascinated by the seemingly endless ways I could manipulate fabrics to create the desired effect. I began to experiment with stitching, stuffing, wrapping, pleating, and cording to form the shapes I needed.

As I took on more challenging projects, I began to search for sturdy but flexible support materials to use as armatures. My local hardware store provided an array of candidates in every shape, form, and configuration I could imagine.

Later on, while working as a designer for a toy manufacturer, I learned simplified methods of sewing and cutting in order to achieve the desired results with the least amount of effort. I have also picked up many shortcuts, tips and techniques along the way from other designers, artists and teachers.

Through the years, I have developed simple and effective methods and materials for creating beautiful gifts, decorative accessories, wearables, and works of art with this exciting and versatile medium.

Inside these pages you will find chapters devoted to the various materials and tools you will need to get started. Furthermore, you will see how the specialized capabilities of Bernina machines offer unique advantages in working with soft sculpture. There are also chapters devoted to helping you learn how to design your own projects from idea to completion.

Finally, I have included a dozen projects of varying levels of complexity with patterns and easy to follow step-by-step instructions for creating a variety of soft sculpted items. I encourage you to learn the techniques through these projects then adapt and modify the design elements to give form to your own ideas.

My ultimate goal in sharing these ideas is to help you discover your own creativity through this fascinating and versatile medium.

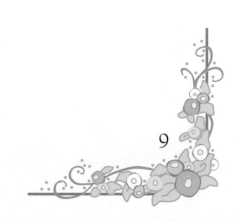

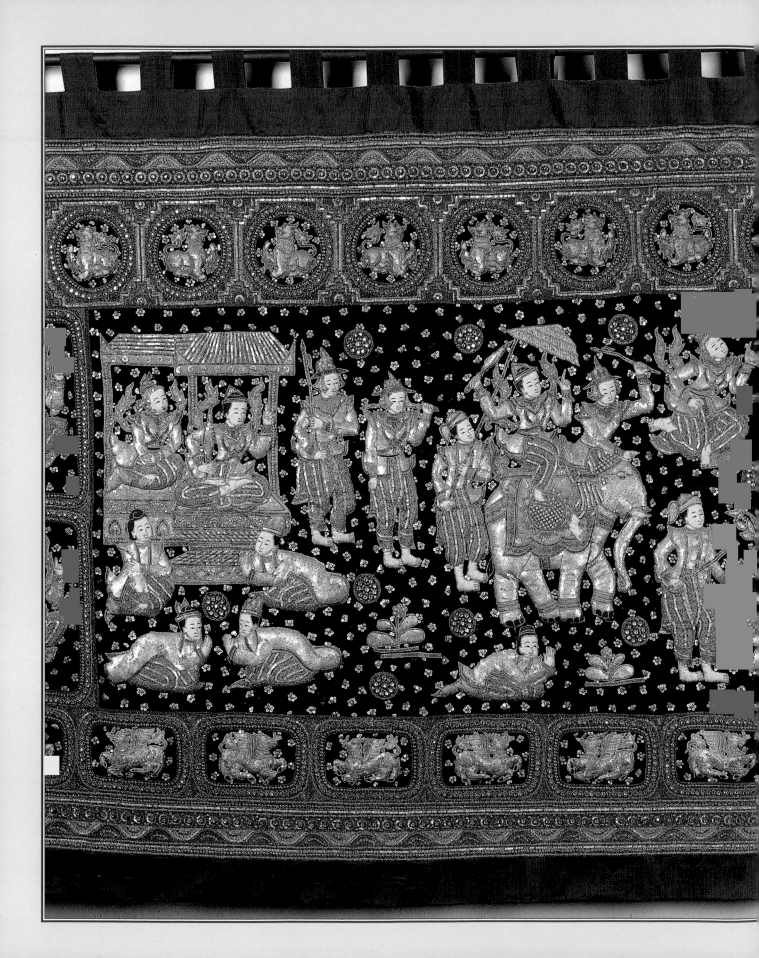

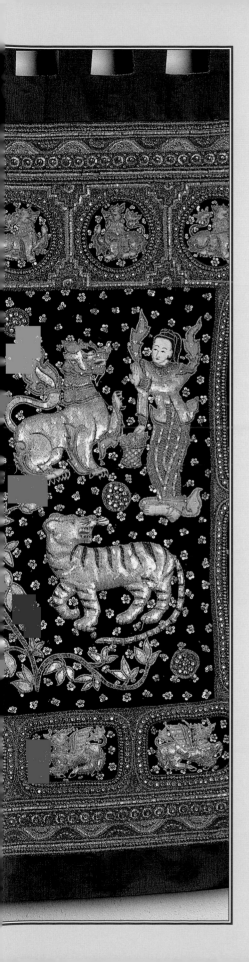

CHAPTER 1

The Origins of Soft Sculpture

*T*hroughout history, in virtually every culture, fibers and textiles have been a principal medium of creative expression. Much of our knowledge of ancient civilizations has been gleaned from small scraps of fabric, dolls and fetishes, ceremonial costumes, and pictorial weaving and tapestries which truly represent the "fabric of our lives."

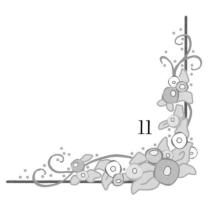

Common Threads

Over the last decade, soft sculpture has gained even more wide-spread popularity as sewing enthusiasts, quilters, and crafters alike have discovered the versatility and appeal of this exciting art form.

Humans seem to create fabrics and textiles as naturally as spiders weave webs and birds build nests. The astounding diversity of ways in which we transform fibers into fabric and fabric into endless varieties of other items is a testimonial to the uniqueness of our individual creativity.

The richly embellished three-dimensional applique wall hanging from Thailand shown in the opening picture of this chapter is called a *kalaga*. Lightly stuffed figures are sewn onto a background fabric which is then virtually covered with complex patterns of hand-sewn beading, sequins, mirrors, and decorative stitches. The tradition of making *kalagas* is thousands of years old and still continues today.

Over the past few decades, as women have gained more freedom to express themselves creatively, they have often turned to the time-honored techniques and everyday materials with which they are familiar. But they have used them in non-traditional ways to explore and expand their creative options. As a result, many of the methods used in traditional sewing crafts such as doll-making, millinery, costuming, quilting, and upholstery have been borrowed, adapted, and synthesized by modern artists and designers into the medium we now call soft sculpture.

Our current fascination with personalizing our home environments has given rise to an explosion of patterns and projects for window treatments, pillows, dolls and other home decor items which feature soft sculpting techniques.

12

These primitive spirit dolls from South America, created
from small scraps of everyday fabric and employing the simplest of
sewing methods, embody that magical quality of intense expression
which connects us to them emotionally, spiritually and intellectually.
From the simplest fetish to the most elaborately costumed doll,
sculpting with fabric has been used by dollmakers around the world
throughout history to give human form to ideas. Children and adults
alike are captivated by this magic.

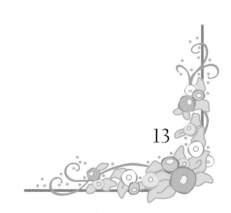

13

Some techniques of soft sculpture were gleaned from upholstered items such as furniture, decorative lampshades, wall hangings, and window cornices, which have traditionally employed elaborate sculptural details including piping, cording, pleating, tufting, and outline quilting.

Today, both the methods and the terminology of upholstery and soft sculpting have become somewhat interchangeable as the category of sewing known as home decor has become an important part of our sewing experience.

Used as an embellishment on apparel, soft sculpture has decorated nearly every imaginable item of clothing from tribal headdresses and ceremonial robes, to royal and clerical vestments and theatrical costumes.

Creators of accessories such as fanciful hats, parasols, handbags and even

14

jewelry have used some of these same fabric sculpting techniques to give dimension to fabrics and trims.

Quiltmaking has played an important role in the spread of soft sculpture as a popular craft among quilters searching for new ways to use their skills. Moving from two to three dimensions seems to be a natural outgrowth of traditional quiltmaking.

The development of modern stabilizers and notions coupled with the inventive use of structural support materials has allowed artists and crafters to create ever more complex and elaborate designs. Furthermore, modern sewing machines and sergers offer many features which facilitate the construction and embellishment of soft sculpted items.

In the next few chapters you will learn about the latest materials, equipment, and techniques available to help you explore this fascinating medium.

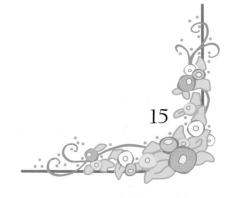

CHAPTER 2

Tools and Materials

Modern innovations in fabrics, notions and equipment have simplified construction of soft sculpture, clearing the way for nearly unbridled creative expression. Products such as fusible interfacing, adhesives, air- and water-soluble marking pens, and innovative stuffing materials have been developed to meet the demands of today's sophisticated sewing enthusiasts who demand excellent results with a minimum of effort.

Sewing Essentials

Fabrics

Many different kinds of fabric are well suited for use in soft sculpture. One of the best sources for fabrics is your own private fabric stash. Collect snippets of richly colored and textured fabrics, paying close attention to weave, pattern, and fabric content. You might personalize your work further by recycling part of a favorite accessory or

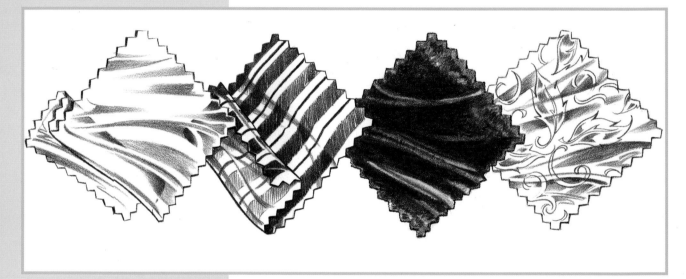

garment. In addition to providing a ready-made, three-dimensional form upon which to build your design, a sleeve from a cashmere sweater, a lovely lace collar or the elegant upturned brim of a felt hat can lend an air of familiarity to your work, as well as giving the viewer a clue to connect with your creative process.

Since soft sculpture appeals to the tactile as well as the visual sense, several factors should be considered when selecting fabrics for your project.

18

Color: Study nature to observe unusual hues and color combinations. Though natural colors and earth tones are generally thought of as somewhat muted, the vibrant contrast between the petals and stamen of a tiny wildflower, or the lusty palette of an exotic insect, can be startlingly beautiful when displayed in the larger context of a soft sculpted piece.

Texture: Contrasting textures can create the illusion of depth and give definition to form by way of light reflected from the surface. Be sure to examine the "wrong" sides of fabrics for additional textures which might be incorporated into the design while maintaining the color scheme.

Pattern: Both woven and printed patterns can be used to enrich the surface of a piece as a metaphor for texture, to emphasize direction, and to delineate shapes and forms. The size of a printed pattern should be in keeping with the overall scale of the project. Consider the subject matter and the distance from which the piece will be viewed to determine the appropriateness of a pattern.

Weight: The weight of a fabric is determined by the closeness of the weave or knit as well as the thickness of the fibers themselves. If additional body or weight is needed, the fabric can be fused to another more sturdy fabric or backed with interfacing. Interesting effects can also be achieved by the overlay of lightweight or transparent fabrics over heavier ones.

Grain/Stretch: Bias cut fabrics are often used to maximize the amount of stretch in a particular fabric. Using bias cut fabrics against straight grain fabrics can produce a dimensional effect when a piece is stuffed. With knitted fabrics, it's important to consider the amount of stretch when fitting pieces together. Using very stretchy fabrics can increase the

19

size of a stuffed piece by two or three times. To minimize stretch, fusible tricot stabilizer can be applied. Interesting textural effects can be obtained when woven and knitted fabrics are used together.

Fabric Content: Fabrics of differing content can often be used together quite effectively to create a desired look. Consider how the piece will be used and if it will have to be laundered before deciding whether to mix fabric contents.

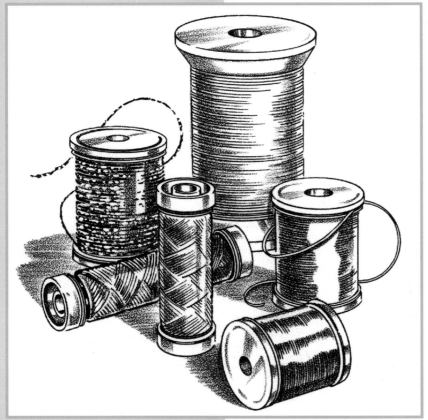

For childrens' rooms and other high traffic areas, washable fabrics such as denim, sweatshirt fleece, parachute nylon, and foam-backed nylon fleece are excellent choices. For more formal pieces, upholstery and drapery fabrics are good choices along with finer fashion fabrics.

Threads

Generally, all-purpose polyester sewing threads are sufficient for construction of most soft sculpture. In certain cases, specialized heavy-duty threads such as hand quilting or upholstery threads may be needed to join large stuffed pieces by hand.

For surface embellishment, rayon embroidery threads, metallic threads and cords, and decorative novelty threads can be used for topstitching, machine quilting, multi-motion decorative stitching, for texturizing fabric, or for couching on trims and braids. Heavier decorative threads and flosses can be wound onto a bobbin and sewn from the wrong side of the fabric to achieve a richly textured surface.

Monofilament fishing line of at least 20–30 lb. strength can be couched onto the cut edge of a stretchy or bias-cut fabric to create a ruffled or "lettuce" edge.

Marking Tools

Careful and accurate marking is crucial to the success of these projects. Several different tools are available for your use.

Air- and water-soluble markers are used to trace around pattern pieces as well as to mark topstitching lines on fabrics.

A chalk wheel marker or a chalk wedge is preferable for darker fabrics.

Iron-on transfer pens are available in many colors. When using, be sure to follow manufacturer's instructions to ensure proper results.

With any marking technique, always test in an inconspicuous place to be sure marks can be removed before marking the fabric surface.

Fusibles and Interfacing

There are numerous recent innovations in interfacing, fusibles, and other sewing aids. These products are essential to the success of soft sculpting as they allow manipulation of the fabric in a variety of ways. Begin collecting a good supply of various weights of woven and nonwoven interfacing, tricot linings, embroidery backing, and fusible webs. Specific uses for these materials will be discussed in detail in later chapters.

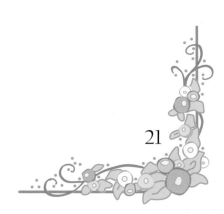

21

Stuffing and Support Tools

It's advisable to become familiar with the various types of commercially available battings and stuffing materials and their capabilities. In addition, recently introduced products such as small polyester pellets can be used to add weight in an area or to create a beanbag effect. For very large pieces, packing peanuts can be used as an effective filler, although they create a somewhat dimpled surface. To counteract this effect, lining with thin batting is recommended.

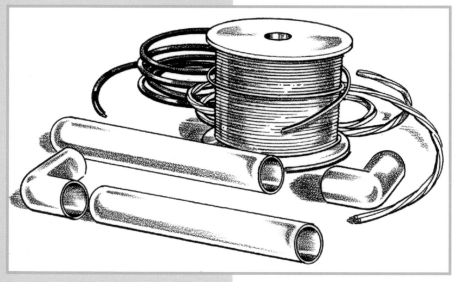

Some pieces will require the additional internal support of an armature. Your local home improvement store can provide some very exciting possibilities when approached from the perspective of a soft sculptor. Foam pipe insulation, wooden dowels, wires, vinyl-covered cable, PVC pipe, wire forms such as a lampshade frame, a tomato cage, a wreath form or a vinyl-covered metal plant stake might yield just the support needed for creating a part. You might also consider recycling some items from around the house such as umbrella stays from a defunct umbrella, coat hanger wire, and so on. For more flexible shapes, foam upholstery padding, cording, and piping are useful.

22

Non-Sewing Tools

23

Several non-sewing tools which might be found around the home are quite useful in creating soft sculpture:

A trigger-feed glue gun is used to join stuffed pieces together.

Needle nose pliers and wire cutters will be needed if wire is used for internal support.

A map measure is a small wheel attached to a gauge which is used to accurately measure the length of a curved line. It is most useful when fitting together two pieces of fabric with unlike shapes. Map measures can be purchased at office supply or stationery stores.

An artist's paintbrush with rather stiff bristles and a long handle is useful for stuffing hard to reach areas. Small bits of stuffing attached to the bristle end are moved easily through the inside of the piece to their final destination. The handle end is used for smoothing stuffing just under the surface of the fabric.

Basic hand tools such as a hammer, saw, and screwdriver may be needed when constructing an armature. Don't worry if your confidence in using these tools is low; armatures by their very definition are not visible in the finished project!

Trims and Embellishments

There are endless possibilities for embellishing the surface and creating points of interest. Ribbon, lace, braid, trim, cord, buttons, beads, small stones, and other items of special interest can be incorporated into a project to personalize it. The techniques for applying various surface embellishments will be discussed in detail in later chapters.

25

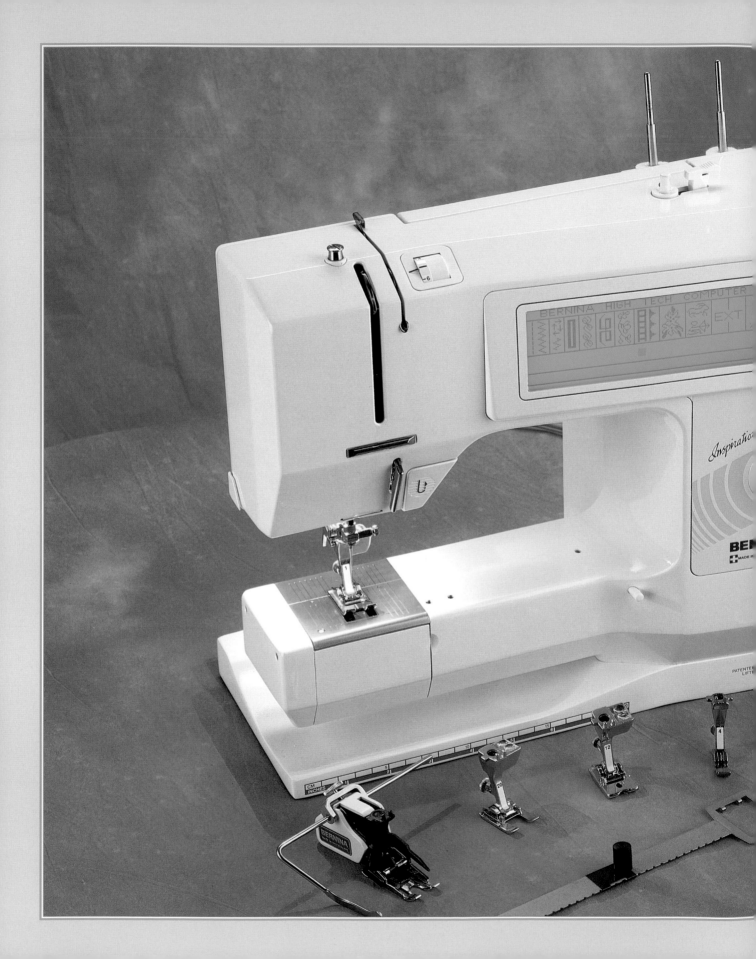

CHAPTER 3

Sewing Machine Features and Accessories

$\mathcal{M}$any of the specialized features found on newer sewing machines offer distinct advantages when working with soft sculpture. Following are a few of the features and accessories which are of special interest to soft sculptors.

27

Features

Soft sculpture can be very labor intensive and your project will have the very best chance of success if you use the best materials, tools and equipment.

It's wise to start each new project or sewing session by examining your needle and changing it if necessary. Choose appropriate needles for the fabrics and threads you are using to ensure the very best results. For detailed information consult your machine's guidebook or your local sewing machine dealer.

Tension adjustment

The tension dial on your sewing machine should be set at a lower number when working with a thick fabric "sandwich"; this loosens the top tension and prevents thread breakage.

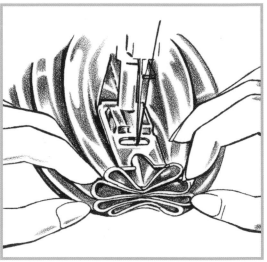

Needle stop up/down

Most newer machines can be set to stop at the end of a stitch or a stitch sequence in the memory with the needle in the up or down position. This feature is quite helpful for pivoting at sharp points and for making precise turns while stitching.

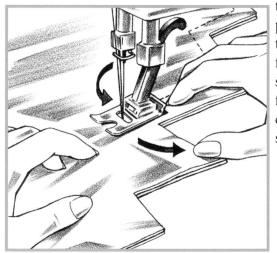

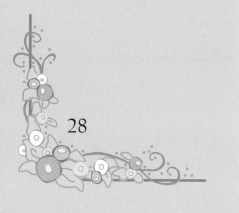

28

Presser foot pressure release knob

Many machines have a knob located on the upper-left corner of the head which controls the pressure on the presser foot. By releasing this pressure and lowering the feed dogs, fabrics can be easily moved manually through the needle area for free-motion sewing.

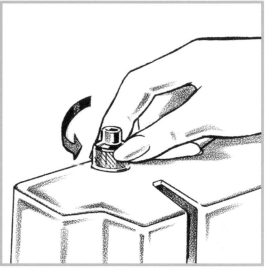

Pre-programmed stitches

Pre-programmed stitch patterns are invaluable for surface embellishment and application of trims and ribbons. Use them liberally to personalize your work. Several can be used to create shapes which can then be cut out in groups, turned and stuffed to create parts as needed.

Long stitch/basting stitch

These functions cause the machine to sew either every second stitch or every fourth stitch and can be used for basting thick layers together or for sewing heavy fabrics. They can also be used for decorative topstitching.

Accessories

Walking foot

The walking foot is used to help feed difficult fabrics, which tend to slip or stick, smoothly through the machine. Used with the seam guide, the walking foot can be invaluable in quilting layers together in a repetitive pattern

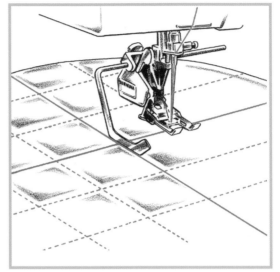

Circular embroidery attachment

If your machine doesn't have a circular embroidery attachment, try the following alternative. Determine the radius of the desired finished circle and then measure from the needle to a left point on the sewing machine bed. Attach a thumbtack to the bed of the sewing machine at that point using cellophane tape. Center the fabric on the thumbtack. The machine will then sew in a circular pattern. This method can be used to create circles and circular patterns of decorative stitches. It has been adapted for a unique soft sculpture application in the beginner project entitled "Cactus Everlasting." Of course, you can always just use an air-soluble marker to mark your circles before sewing.

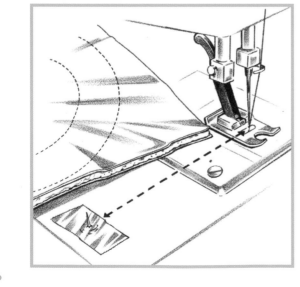

30

Leather roller foot

A leather roller foot is handy for sewing together layers of heavy and stiff fabrics such as leather, vinyl and suede. Be sure to use a leather needle with it for best results.

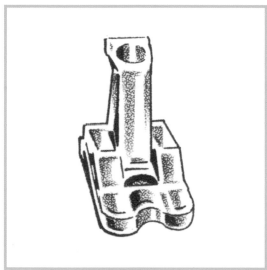

Cording foot

This foot is invaluable for creating and applying corded piping and braided trims. It has a deep groove on the underside which rides over the braid to ensure smooth application by aligning the braid or cord very close to the stitching line.

Open-toe embroidery foot

This foot is best used for surface embellishment and satin stitching. It provides maximum visibility at the point where the needle enters the fabric. When using any open-toe foot, hold fabric taut or use embroidery hoops for best results.

31

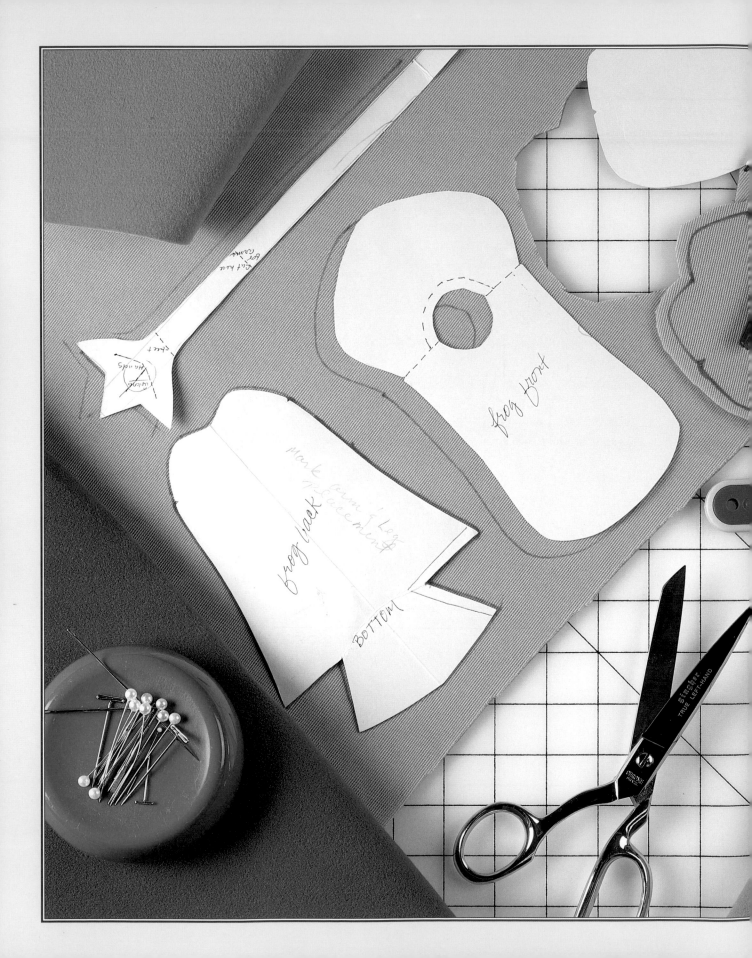

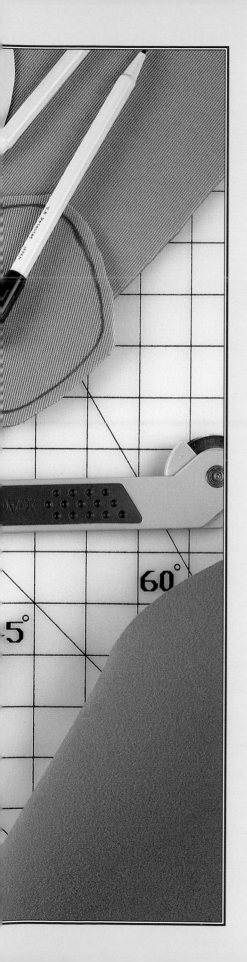

CHAPTER 4

How to Work with Patterns

*S*oft sculpture differs from fashion sewing in that there is no right or wrong way to fit things together. The projects in this book were designed to familiarize you with several ways of working with patterns such as: template tracing, pattern pieces with seam allowances included, draping, and special pattern layouts to save cutting and construction time. Using these techniques and unique fabric preparations guarantee optimum results.

33

Pattern Tips

Transferring patterns onto fabric

A shortcut for creating two-layer shapes is to cut a template for the pattern pieces out of pattern board or acetate.

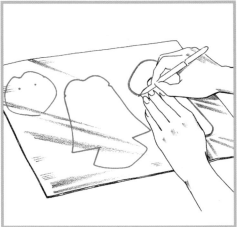

Complete patterns for all projects in this book can be found inside the front and back covers. Trace patterns for your project onto tracing paper, transferring all markings, then copy onto stiff pattern cardboard or clear acetate sheets to create durable patterns. (Note: When copying onto acetate, use a permanent marking pen.)

A template is cut to the exact shape of the finished piece without added seam allowances. Then, using an air-soluble marker, trace around the outside edges of the template to mark the exact stitching lines. The pieces are sewn together *before* you cut them out. Be sure to read each instruction completely before cutting.

In other cases, the seam allowances have been included on the patterns. These stitching lines are clearly marked with a broken line, usually inside the cutting line. This construction method is used when sewing dissimilar pieces together or when special indicators are necessary.

A third method of construction involves dimensional measurements. The instructions might read "cut a 10"x12" rectangle" or "cut a 6" circle." Accurate measuring is crucial to the success of all projects.

Draping

In the advanced projects, draping will be used to determine fabric shapes. Draping, a fashion design technique adapted here for soft sculpture, involves placing fabric directly onto an armature and pinning in place to ensure proper fit.

34

Interlocking pattern layout

When transferring patterns to fabric, leave enough space between shapes for seam allowances. A good rule of thumb for most fabrics is ½" between shapes so that when the sewn shapes are cut apart a ¼" seam allowance remains. Often the shapes can be arranged on the fabrics so that one cut creates two seam allowances.

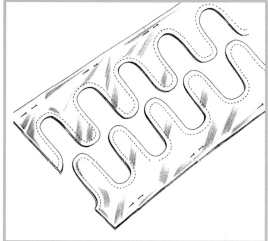

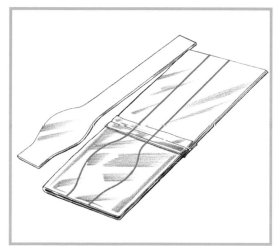

Color blocking

Another fashion design technique adapted for use in soft sculpture projects is color blocking. Contrasting fabrics are assembled before pattern pieces are traced to simplify cutting and construction.

Fusing fabrics together

Fabrics are fused together for strength or to create specialized combinations of colors or textures. Fusible tricot interfacing added to a knit fabric reduces stretch or prevents fraying on woven fabrics. It adds body without changing the essential characteristics of the fabric or adding weight. Two-toned double-faced fabrics are created by fusing together wrong sides of contrasting fabrics. Always follow manufacturer's fusing instructions carefully to ensure success and prevent damage to fabrics.

35

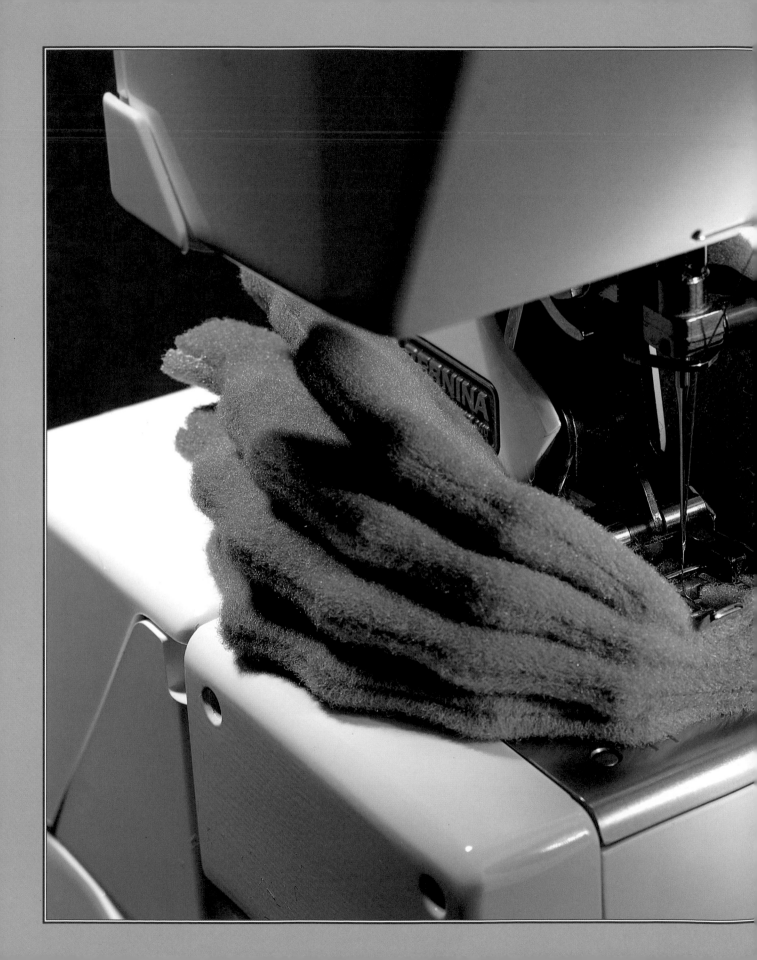

CHAPTER 5

Shortcuts and Specialized Sewing Techniques

*I*n this chapter you will learn some techniques and shortcuts which have been developed or adapted specifically for soft sculpting. These methods for stitching, turning, stuffing and joining will simplify the process of construction and in many cases ensure the success of your projects.

Specialized Tips

The following techniques are used on many of the projects in this book. Familiarize yourself with this information before beginning any project.

Circular stitching

A circular embroidery attachment consists of a ruler-like arm that extends from the left of the presser foot across the bed of the sewing machine. An adjustable slide with a small spike attached is used to pierce the fabric at a chosen center point forming a radius with the machine needle. Once stitching begins, the fabric moves through the machine in a circular motion.

If a circular embroidery attachment is not available for your machine, use a thumbtack, point facing up, and measure the appropriate radius distance from the needle to the tack for the size of circle to be sewn. Attach the tack to the bed of the machine with strong tape. Position the center of the fabric on the tack and proceed with circular stitching.

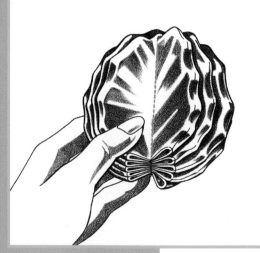

Stack and stitch

A unique method for creating three-dimensional forms is to stack several layers of sewn, turned but unstuffed shapes, matching the edges very carefully. Stitch through all layers to form a series of channels which will fill out to become a round form when stuffed. A walking foot is helpful to prevent shifting.

Sewing, then cutting

When a project requires several small shapes, stitch completely around each piece and then cut out all the sewn shapes at once simplifying sewing and shortening cutting time.

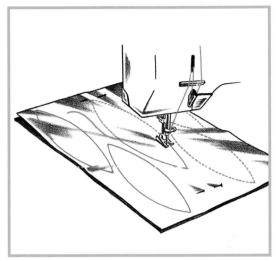

Topstitching and free-motion quilting

A lightly filled shape or one lined with batting can be topstitched to create a dimensional or quilted effect. Lengthen the stitch slightly to accommodate the layers of fabric and batting. Pin the layers together carefully to avoid shifting while sewing. Use a free-motion or quilting foot and lower the feed dogs to draw patterns with needle and thread across the fabric surface. Natural textures of leaves or bark are easily created.

Linear quilting

When working with bulky fabrics and multiple layers, use a walking foot to move fabric easily through the machine and prevent shifting while sewing. Attach and adjust guides to facilitate stitching of parallel rows.

Flat joining seams

To join curved edges of two pieces of fabric without adding the bulk of a seam allowance, set the machine to a narrow zig zag stitch. Using a monofilament thread, butt edges and center under presser foot. Stitch carefully, adjusting edges while sewing to accommodate curves.

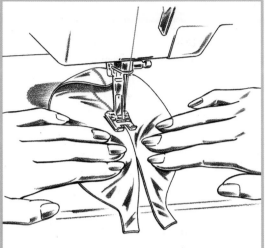

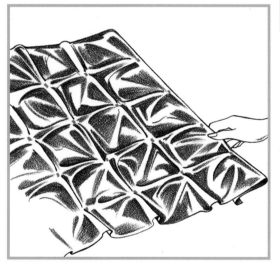

Gathering

For easy gathering, set machine to a narrow, long, zig zag stitch and sew over nylon upholstery thread. Use a cording foot, if available, to keep upholstery thread centered between zig zag stitches. Pull nylon thread to gather. This method prevents broken threads and makes adjusting the fullness of gathers easier.

Pleating and tucking

Manipulating fabric by pleating or tucking adds texture, pattern, and stability. Fold and press pleats or tucks and secure with bartacks or topstitching. The topstitching or bartacking can be integrated as a design element.

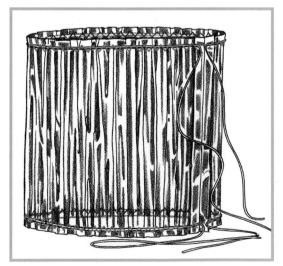

40

Tips for turning

For professional-looking results, always notch inside curves and clip outside curves close to the stitching line. Trim away excess fabric from points. Use a point turner or paint brush handle to open out each point or appendage before stuffing. When turning tubes, stitch across one end to close, then insert a dowel or turning rod to turn from the closed end. When turning a sewn shape right side out, always start from the point farthest from the opening for ease in turning.

Slash and turn

When working with two-layer shapes, stitch completely around the outside of the shape along the marked stitching line. Slit the shape in the back or in an inconspicuous place for turning and stuffing. The integrity of the shape is maintained and the slit can then be whipstitched closed.

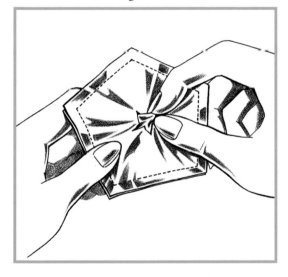

Stuffing

Stuffing is a crucial and integral part of soft sculpting. Care should be taken in the selection and application of materials and methods. Densely packed stuffing produces a firm free-standing object, whereas lightly stuffed objects tend to be more flexible and may need the additional support of an armature.

Polyester fiberfill is available in two styles, one very soft and fluffy while the other produces a more dense, solid effect. Natural fiber stuffing, such as cotton and kapok, produces slightly different effects. Experiment to see which suits the needs of your project. To remove a dimpled or lumpy appearance, run a paint brush handle under fabric surface to distribute stuffing evenly, or, if necessary, line with a thin layer of quilt batting.

For flatter pieces, layers of batting can be placed under the fabrics before sewing to simplify stuffing. Choose batting of appropriate thickness and density to vary depth and firmness. Always trim batting close to stitching lines to avoid bulkiness around seams. Topstitching though all layers will stabilize the batting and create a trapunto effect.

To add weight to certain areas for stability or to create posable shapes, polyester pellets can be used alone or with other stuffing materials. These small pellets are durable, easy to use and widely available. For ease of insertion, use a funnel or drinking straw to deposit pellets evenly and neatly.

Pressing

As with fashion sewing, "pressing as you go" yields professional results in soft sculpting. Use an iron to form and re-shape sewn pieces. Heat and steam can be used to set folds and pleats prior to assembly.

42

Gluing

The glue gun has enabled soft sculptors to eliminate much of the hand sewing previously required in joining pieces. The ease of application and instant bonding make it preferable to other gluing methods. It can be used for fabric-to-fabric bonds, as well as joining unlike materials.

Apply glue carefully to one surface and hold in place against the other surface for at least one minute to ensure a tight bond. For best results, use a trigger feed gun if available.

(Note: To remove excess glue, or separate previously glued pieces, heat area briefly with a hair dryer to soften bond and lift glue from surface.) *Safety tip: Keep a glass of ice water nearby when working with a glue gun. Should you accidentally touch the glue to your fingertips, immerse fingers immediately to cool the glue and avoid burns.*

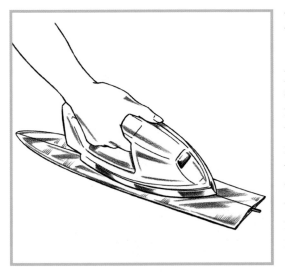

Fusing after sewing

One unique fusing application presented in this book is fusible web applied after sewing. Once stitching is completed, fusible web is applied to one side prior to turning. The backing is removed, the piece is turned right side out and a stabilizing wire is inserted. Heat is then applied again to fuse the two pieces and permanently set the wire in place. For best results, always follow manufacturer's instructions and recommendations carefully.

CHAPTER 6

Finishing Touches

Finishing touches such as beading, embroidery, surface manipulation, and trims can transform the ordinary into the extraordinary. Explore, experiment and give over your imagination to the possibilities. You will be rewarded for your efforts with the ultimate in creative expression.

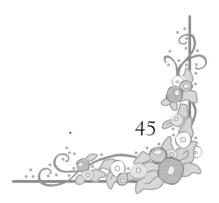

45

Additional Embellishment

Cords, trims, and tassels

These additional techniques add the final creative embellishment to the projects listed in this book.

Knotting cords and trims to produce three-dimensional components for soft sculpture is borrowed from traditional macramé techniques. Fraying cords and braids to create tassels and flower centers also incorporates these elements into your work. Recycling braids, trims and cords from other projects provides endless possibilities for embellishment. Glue, handstitch, wrap or tie them to create points of visual interest.

Braids and cords can be couched onto fabrics at seams to emphasize structural lines, or in an allover pattern for added textural effects. Select a braiding foot, a narrow zig zag or other decorative stitch of your choice. Test a small area first as this method tends to stiffen the fabric. Adapt this technique to couch wire for added stability or shaping.

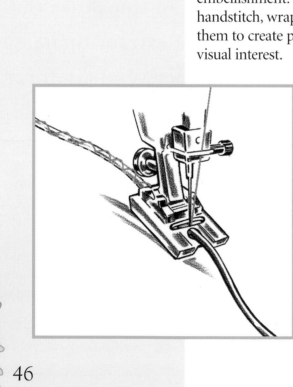

46

Decorative machine embroidery

Dozens of stitch options and unlimited thread choices are available to decorate and clean-finish fabrics, create textures and patterns, or add color. Specialized presser feet and pre-programmed stitches produce the look of opulent hand embroidery effortlessly. Use perforated embroidery backing under fabrics to stabilize and rayon embroidery threads for guaranteed success.

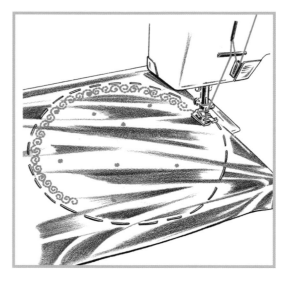

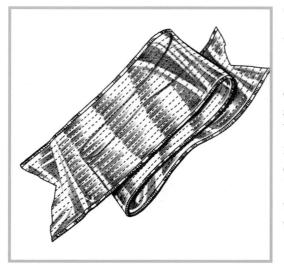

Topstitching to create texture

Parallel rows of straight stitching can enhance the surface of fabrics by adding texture and creating realistic effects. When used as a quilting technique, it mimics traditional trapunto. Specialized double needles are available in several sizes (for example, 2.0mm indicating the distance between the needles). Two spools of thread and one bobbin are required.

47

Wrapping

Wrapping fabric or trim around a form is an effective way to cover it or create texture. Overlapping wrapped layers slightly prevents fraying, adds dimension, and simulates true-to-life growth patterns.

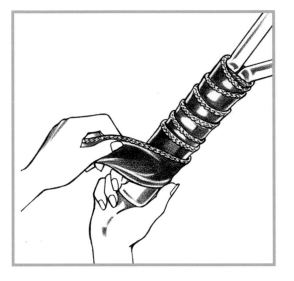

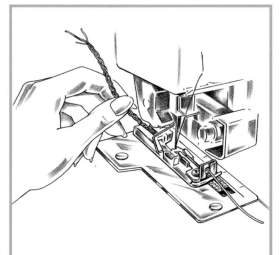

Serged wire edge

Wire-edged ribbons, available in many colors, widths, and fabrications are the soft sculptor's dream. The wire edges function as an internal armature so the ribbon can be easily sculpted, reshaped and retain its form indefinitely.

To create your own wire-edged ribbons and trims, select the cording foot and decorative thread and adjust the serger for a three-thread rolled edge. Insert wire into the foot and serge edges of fabric to create wire-edged ribbon or trim.

Hand embellishment

Hand embellishment or nontraditional stitching techniques, and manipulation of diverse fibers and colors can produce unexpected, spectacular results and add a personal touch to your work.

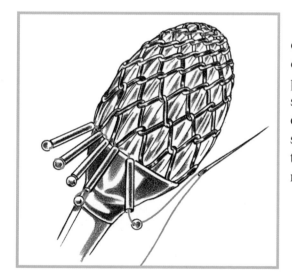

Beads, buttons, small stones, and other treasured items or trinkets add special sparkle, create points of interest, and personalize your work. Beads come in all shapes, sizes and colors, offering limitless opportunities for creative expression. Use special beading needles and beading thread to ensure durability. Apply carefully, reinforcing knots.

49

CHAPTER 7

Beginner Projects

*U*sing the very simplest of techniques and a minimum of effort, you can transform an entire room, embellish your clothing or create unique gifts and accessories. The diverse projects described in this chapter utilize techniques which will give you a strong foundation of basic skills for soft sculpting.

MATERIALS:

- foam-backed nylon fleece, sweatshirt fleece or stretch velour fabric
- polyester fiberfill (letters)
- polyester high loft batting (headboard)
- 1½" diam upholstery cording (headboard)
- 30" woven nylon cord for each balloon letter (wallhanging)
- small plastic rings for hanging (wallhanging)
- air-soluble marker
- matching thread
- general sewing equipment

TECHNIQUES:

Transferring patterns onto fabric, page 34
Sewing, then cutting, page 39
Slash and turn, page 41
Topstitching and free-motion quilting, page 39
Stuffing, pages 41-42

MEASURING:

Cut two 10" squares of foam-backed nylon fleece for each letter

Alphabet Child's Room

*T*hese brightly-colored sculpted alphabet letters can be used to create an entire child's room decorative ensemble including wallhanging, throw pillows and even a headboard. They could even dance across a padded valance for a unique window treatment.

52

Instructions:

1. Place pattern right side up on double thickness of fabric right sides together. Trace outline onto fabric using air-soluble marker.

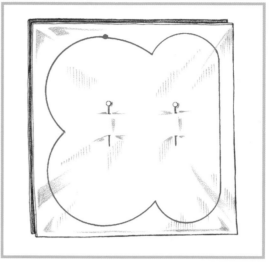

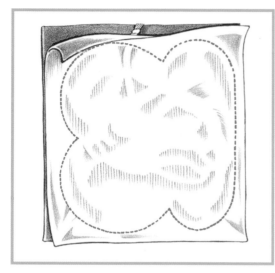

2. Stitch completely around outline. For balloon wallhanging, insert cord at dot. Stitch securely in place positioning cord inside letter. Cut out letters leaving ¼" seam allowances.

3. Place letter in readable postion and slit top layer along slit line. Turn right side out opening seams fully.

4. Place pattern over letters and mark top-stitching lines with air-soluble marker. Topstitch over all markings. Stuff lightly with polyester fiberfil. Whip stitch closed.

5. Finish as wallhanging by sewing small plastic rings as hangers on back.

6. To finish as twin headboard, cover headboard with layer of batting. Make oversized cording to fit around sides and top of padded headboard. Pin cording along seamline on right side of one layer of fabric. Stitch along seamline with zipper foot. Place other layer of fabric on top of corded layer right sides together. Pin in place. Stitch close to cording using zipper foot. Turn right side out. Finish lower edge. Glue to headboard with glue gun.

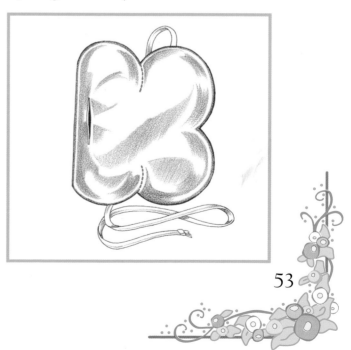

53

MATERIALS:

- foam-backed fleece, or velour or sweatshirt fleece with fusible knit backing applied, green and rust
- polyester fiberfill
- air-soluble marking pen
- glue gun
- invisible nylon monofil or matching polyester thread
- circular embroidery attachment
- general sewing equipment

TECHNIQUES:

Sewing, then cutting, page 39
Circular stitching, page 38
Slash and turn, page 41
Stack and stitch, page 38
Tips for turning, page 41
Stuffing, pages 41-42

MEASURING:

For each individual cactus plant you will need eight or ten squares of fabric 1½" larger than the diameter of the circle size you select. For the cactus garden shown, 10", 8", 6", 5", and 4" squares were used. For the small individual potted cactus, eight 4" squares were used. To make each cactus flower, two 4" squares were used.

54

Cactus Everlasting

*T*hese realistic looking cacti will make an attractive addition to any casual decor. They are so easy to make and best of all, never need watering! Group several together in clay pots or colorful baskets, or if you prefer, pot each one individually for use as a pin cushion. They are easy to make, and fun to give.

Instructions:

1. With right sides facing, center two fabric squares on circular embroidery device and attach to spike. Set machine to sew a long scallop stitch, and stitch around circle. For this project it is not crucial that the scallops join together because the bottoms of the circles will be left open for stuffing purposes.

2. If you are making several cacti, sew all the large size circles at once then reset the tack to alter the size of the sewing radius and sew the next smallest circles.

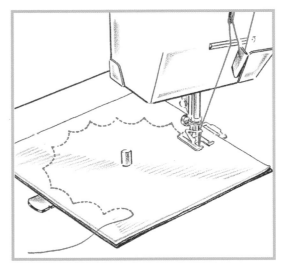

3. Trim, clip curves and trim away fabric from lower edge of circle to leave an opening at least 2½" across for stuffing.

4. Turn each circle right side out and use point turner to completely turn out each of the points of the scallops.

5. Use an air-soluble marker to mark through the center of one turned segment from top to bottom. Stack segments with marked segment on top, carefully matching edges. Stitch through center of all segments beginning with a securing stitch ½" from top.

6. Stuff lightly with polyester fiberfill, filling each section a little at a time until cactus is fully rounded. Use a stuffing tool or paint brush handle to guide fiberfill into farthest points. Leave approximately ½" at the lower edge of each section empty. It is not necessary to sew sections closed if you plan to permanently glue the cactus into a container.

7. To make cactus flowers, use two 4" squares for each flower and attach to circular embroidery attachment at smallest setting. Sew all the way around circle, adjusting scallops as necessary near the end so that they meet. Clip a small X in center of one layer to turn flower right side out.

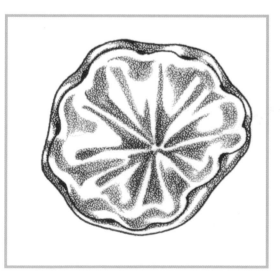

56

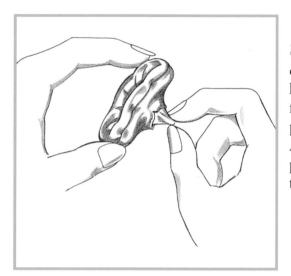

8. Do not turn out points fully. Push center of upper layer through cut in lower layer and pull through slightly to gather flower. To secure flower center, hand stitch point to clipped edge at center back. Arrange cacti in basket or pot and glue in place. Use glue to attach flowers to center tops of cacti.

MATERIALS:

- foam-backed nylon fleece fabric
- polyester pellets
- polyester fiberfill
- lock-in animal eyes
- Velcro® hook fastener dots
- matching thread
- general sewing supplies
- air-soluble marker

TECHNIQUES:

Transferring patterns onto fabric, page 34
Sewing, then cutting, page 39
Slash and turn, page 41
Stuffing, pages 41-42

MEASURING:

Tracing and measuring information is included within the project instruction.

Frog Family Fun

his trio of whimsical frog characters will delight children (and adults!) of all ages. A new take on classic beanbag toys, they are sculpted from a foam-backed fleece fabric which attracts hook type fastening tape. Velcro® hook fastener dots on the hands and accessories facilitate gesturing and costume changes for hours of fun. Polyester pellets weight the body and feet for ease in posing.

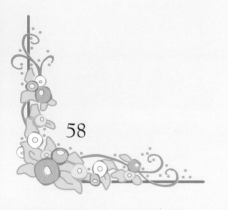

58

Instructions:

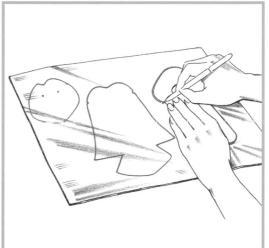

1. To make body/head, trace pattern templates onto wrong sides of one layer of fabric. These patterns include ¼" seam allowances. Cut out along traced lines. To make arms and legs, trace arm and leg templates onto double layer of fabric right sides facing.

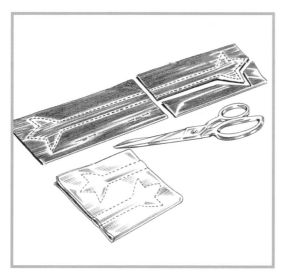

2. Stitch along traced lines then cut out leaving ¼" seam allowance. Turn.

3. For hands, top stitch hook tape to one side of hands following stitching guide. Begin at wrist and make double row of stitches to each "finger" and back to center to secure hook tape and create sculpted effect on hands.

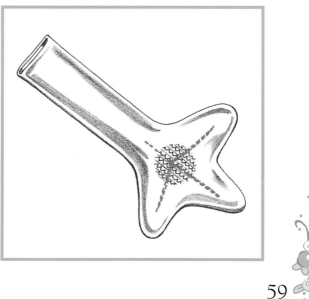

4. To make legs, fill feet with polyester pellets. Insert a large diameter drinking straw through leg all the way into foot area. Use straw to scoop pellets into foot. Fill foot completely then sew across foot to secure.

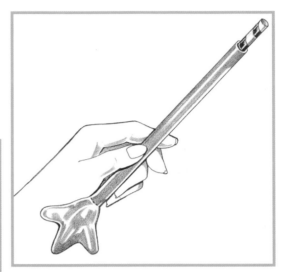

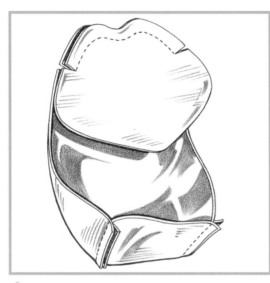

5. Stitch darts in frog back. Sew frog head to frog back above notches.

6. Fold frog front along dotted line, right sides together. Stitch around one half of the circle to form chin dart.

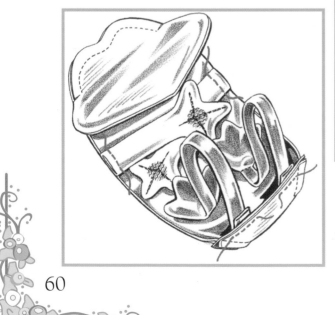

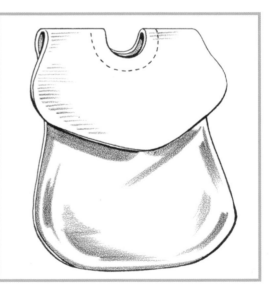

7. Baste hands and feet in place onto body back.

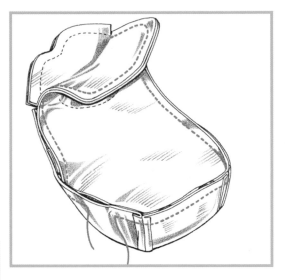

8. Match front to back/head at notches, right sides facing and stitch together, leaving open below one arm to turn.

9. Turn right side out. Attach lock-in eyes following manufacturer's instructions.

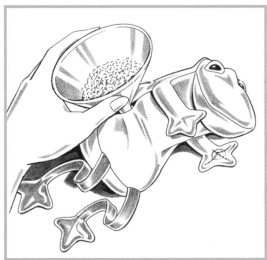

10. Insert small kitchen funnel into opening and fill lower body with polyester pellets. Stuff remainder of body with polyester fiberfill being careful not to overstuff frog under chin. Slip stitch opening closed.

11. To make the bow tie or mom's bodice, use an air-soluble marker to trace around the pattern template onto a double layer of fabric right sides facing. Sew completely around the marked outline. Cut out, leaving a $\frac{1}{4}$" seam allowance. Cut a small slit in the center of one side and turn right side out.

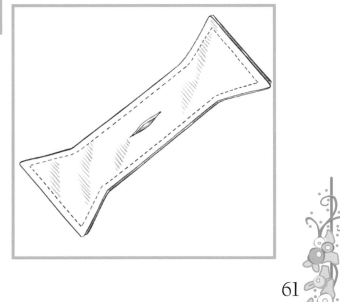

61

12. With slit to inside, tie a knot in center of bow tie/bodice, adjusting as necessary to equalize ends. Center Velcro® hook dots on both sides of bow tie back and hand sew in place. (Note: The back side of the bow has the flat side of the knot.)

13. To make the dad's tie, use an air-soluble marker to trace around the pattern template onto a double thickness of fabric, right sides facing. Sew around tie leaving open at top.

Cut out leaving ¼" seam allowance.

14. Turn in raw edges at top and hand sew closed. Tie knot at top and hand sew Velcro© hook dot onto knot.

62

15. To make the baby's bonnet, a bib, or an apron, use an air-soluble marker to trace around the pattern template onto a double thickness of fabric, right sides facing. Sew completely around, leaving open at one end to turn. Stitch again between dots for ease in turning.

16. Cut out leaving ¼" seam allowance. Use a paint brush to turn right side out beginning with opposite end. Turn in raw edges and slipstitch closed. Sew Velcro® hook dot as indicated on pattern template.

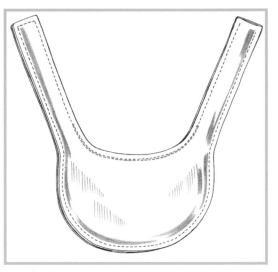

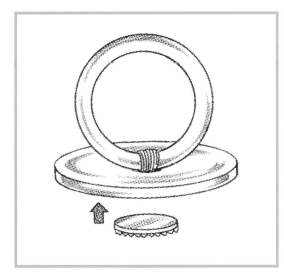

17. To make the baby's pacifier, use a 1" button with two holes and a ¾" plastic ring. Sew ring very securely to button, using upholstery weight nylon thread or dental floss. Glue Velcro® hook dot to back, covering knot.

Safety tip: This item is small and could pose a choking hazard to very small children and babies. Keep from their reach.

18. To make the skirt, cut a rectangle 12" x 4". Sew ends together to form cylinder. Turn up ½" hem along bottom edge. Machine stitch ⅜" from fold.

19. Repeat same process along upper edge to form casing, leaving open to insert ¼" elastic. Machine stitch closed.

63

MATERIALS:

- purchased straw hat
- $\frac{1}{8}$ yd moire or satin fabric for flowers
- $\frac{1}{4}$ yd moire or satin fabric for band and stems
- $\frac{1}{4}$ yd tulle
- 3 yds ombre wire-edged ribbon
- $\frac{2}{3}$ yd yellow rattail cord for flower centers
- 1 piece florist wire or chenille stem
- glue gun

TECHNIQUES:

Transferring patterns onto fabric, page 34
Sewing, then cutting, page 39
Slash and turn, page 41
Tips for turning, page 41

MEASURING:

Trace violet template three times onto double thickness of fabric, right sides facing, leaving at least $\frac{1}{2}$" between shapes. Cut a 1"-wide, 12"-long strip of green fabric. Cut rattail cord into three 8" lengths.

Victorian Violet Hat

*A*n inexpensive plain straw hat has been magically transformed into this lovely Victorian creation with the addition of a simple band, a bit of netting, a small cluster of soft sculpted violets and some artfully arranged wire edged ribbon.

64

Instructions:

1. Stitch completely around each shape along marked outlines. Cut apart leaving ¼" seam allowances.

2. Cut a small X in center of each flower for turning. Press.

3. Fold green strip lengthwise, right sides together. Sew ¼" from folded edge and across one end to create stems. Turn. Cut into thirds.

4. Tie two knots in the center of each piece of rattail, one over the other for flower centers. Glue ends to small length of florist wire.

5. Insert wire through center of flower. Pull to underside. Slip stem over wire. Glue in place.

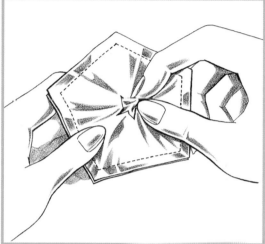

6. Make hat band from green fabric, tying knot in center back. Glue in place on hat.

7. Shape 1 yard of ribbon into multi-looped bow. Glue at center back. Intertwine another 1 yard of ribbon loosely around hat, using photo as guide. Crimp ribbon to create dimensional look.

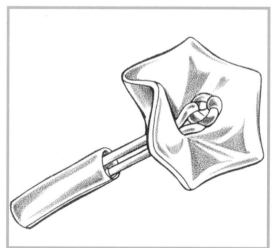

8. Shape remaining ribbon around fingers creating loops. Pinch together. Bring two edges together to form leaf centers. Flatten slightly. Create cluster of leaves in this manner. Glue in to side of hat near front. Glue violets over leaves, tucking in ends under band. Accent band with tulle, securing with glue as needed.

65

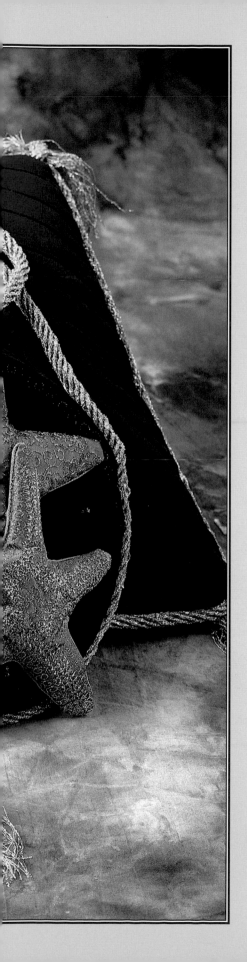

Intermediate Projects

*I*nspired by Mother Nature, the projects in this chapter are designed to broaden your technical knowledge while stretching your imagination. Building upon the skills gained in Chapter 7, we have added structural support materials and embellishment techniques to yield extraordinary results.

MATERIALS:

- foam-backed fleece fabric, camel, 30" x 60"
- foam-backed fleece fabric, raspberry, 15" x 15"
- fusible fleece batting, 15" x 32"
- fusible web, 6" x 6"
- rayon embroidery thread
- 3 raspberry-colored buttons (berries)
- 1" piece tan hook fastener tape
- air-soluble marker
- point turner
- general sewing equipment
- matching thread

TECHNIQUES:

Circular stitching, page 38
Decorative machine embroidery, page 47
Linear quilting, page 39
Fusing fabrics together, page 35
Tips for turning, page 41

MEASURING:

Cut two 15" circles, two 10" circles and two side crust pieces from camel fabric. Cut twelve strips, ¾" x 12" from camel fabric. Fuse together two layers camel fabric and cut three leaves. Cut one 11" circle from raspberry fabric.

68

All-American Pie Cozy

Y ou will create quite a stir at the next potluck dinner when you present your favorite fresh-from-the-oven homemade pie nestled in this scrumptious looking berry pie cozy. Trompe l'oeil woven lattice crust, sculpted pastry leaves and button berries create the look of down home goodness. This technique could also be adapted to create a delightfully whimsical pillow top.

Instructions:

1. To make the fluted crust, mark center of 15" circles and attach circular embroidery attachment or use thumb tack set at 6½" radius. Set machine for an elongated reverse scallop stitch. With right sides together, stitch around circle. Trim close to stitching. Notch seam allowance. With air-soluble marker, mark another circle 1½" inside outer edge. Cut along this line through one thickness only.

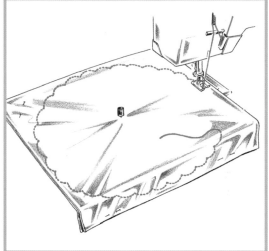

2. Turn right side out and use point turner to push out scallops.

3. Center on circular attachment with radius of 6" and topstitch with straight stitch to form crust edge. Remove from attachment and edgestitch inside cut edge using decorative edging stitch of choice.

4. To make lattice top, using all-purpose presser foot, edge stitch both sides of all 12" strips, using the same decorative edging stitch chosen previously. Arrange strips on raspberry circle and weave together to form lattice top. Secure with pins. Baste stitch near outer edge. Trim to fit circle. Center lattice top inside fluted crust. Secure with pins. Topstitch ¼" from inside edge of crust using the walking foot with guide and straight stitch.

69

5. To make bottom crust, trim ½" seam allowance from fusible fleece batting and fuse to wrong side of one 10" circle. Pin circles together with right sides out. Using air soluble marker, draw intersecting lines through center of circle. Set walking foot guide on 1". Stitch over marked lines at 1" intervals from center marks with straight stitch to form quilted grid pattern. Trim threads.

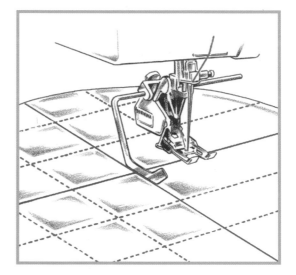

6. To make side crust, trim away seam allowance from fusible fleece batting and fuse to one side crust piece. Stitch ends of side crusts to form two circles. Press seams open. With right sides together, place one inside the other offsetting seams to eliminate bulk. Stitch around upper edge. Trim close. Turn and press. Sew hook tape at seam near upper inside edge only.

7. Topstitch at ⅞" from upper edge through all thicknesses to form lip.

8. Pin bottom and sides, right sides together, and stitch carefully avoiding puckers. Trim seam to ¼". Clean-finish seam with overcast stitch.

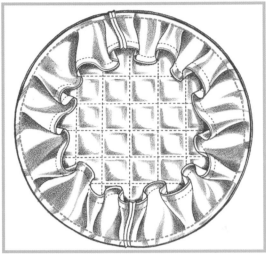

9. To make the leaves, select embroidery foot and decorative edging stitch of choice. Edgestitch leaves starting at one point and turning at other end.

10. Set the machine for straight stitch. Fold leaves lengthwise and stitch dart as shown to form dimensional leaves. Arrange on lattice with buttons as berries and sew by hand to attach.

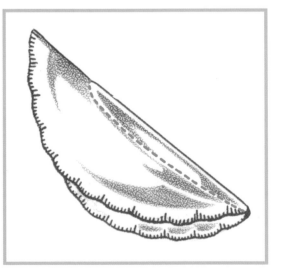

MATERIALS:

Starfish

- ⅓ yd gold metallic organza
- ⅓ yd gold satin fabric
- polyester fiberfill
- gold metallic thread
- 8" machine embroidery hoop
- air-soluble marker
- 12" of thin gold braided cord for hanging

Evening Bag

- ⅓ yd deep blue velvet fabric
- ⅓ yd lining fabric
- 2 yds heavy gold braided cording for shoulder strap
- ⅓ yd polyester batting
- 1 large covered snap

Dream Pillow

- ½ yd blue faille or silk-like fabric
- ½ yd fusible tricot interfacing
- ½ yd polyester batting
- 1 polyester pillow form
- blue rayon embroidery thread to match fabric
- 2½ yds heavy gold braided cording
- double needle

72

Starfish Ornament, Evening Bag and Dream Pillow

*R*ecreate nature's star of wonder. Recall the waves, the sand, the mystery of starlit nights. Gather this trio of golden starfish to bejewel an evening bag, twinkle on your Christmas tree or dance across your dream pillow. Machine embroidered metallic threads give these jewels of the sea their rich texture.

Instructions:

Starfish

TECHNIQUES:

Decorative machine embroidery, page 47
Transferring patterns onto fabric, page 34
Sewing, then cutting, page 39
Tips for turning, page 41
Slash and turn, page 41
Stuffing, pages 41-42
Topstitching to create texture, page 47

MEASURING:

Tracing and measuring information is included within each starfish project instruction.

1. Layer organza on top of satin fabric right sides up in embroidery hoop so the two pieces are smooth and taut. Trace around starfish template using air-soluble marker. Using metallic thread, apply decorative stitches following general shape of starfish, overlapping slightly to assure complete coverage.

2. Remove fabric from embroidery hoop, place on layer of satin fabric, right sides together, and trace template on wrong side of stitched starfish shape. Stitch completely around outline.

3. Cut out starfish leaving ¼" seam allowance. Trim off excess fabric at points. Cut a small slit in center back and turn right side out.

4. Use a point turner or paint brush handle to completely turn out points.

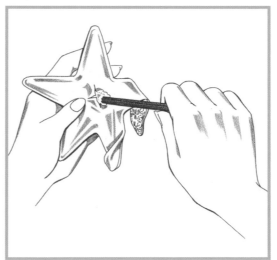

5. Stuff with polyester fiberfill. Hand sew slit closed.

CHAPTER 8 — *Intermediate Projects*

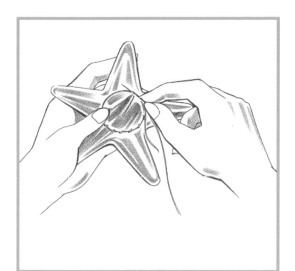

6. Cut a small piece of fabric large enough to fit over slit, turn under edges and slipstitch in place.

Evening Bag

1. Place a layer of quilt batting on wrong side of velvet and trace two bag templates. Baste two layers together along outline with contrasting thread.

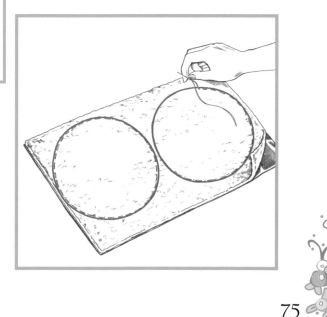

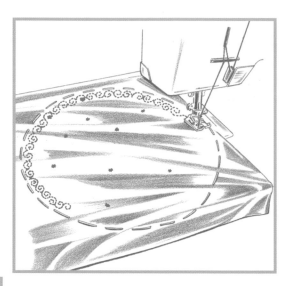

$2.$ With velvet side up and using decorative metallic thread, apply decorative stitching around inside edge of circles, placing edge of presser foot along basting line. Then, randomly stitch single star pattern all over both pieces. Cut out circles ½" beyond basting lines.

$3.$ Trace and cut two bag templates from lining fabric. Mark notches. With right sides together, sew lining pieces to velvet pieces between notches only, as indicated on pattern. Notch and trim seam allowances.

$4.$ Pin velvet circles together and lining circles together and stitch each between notches, leaving lining open for turning. Notch, trim and turn. Slipstitch lining closed.

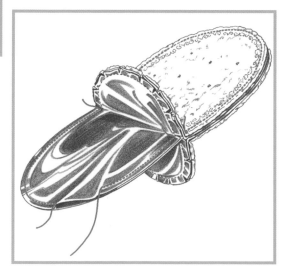

76

5. With contrasting decorative thread, slipstitch lining to seam allowance around inside of bag opening to prevent lining from rolling to the outside. Sew nylon snap to inside of opening keeping lining free from velvet.

6. Measure desired length of gold cord for shoulder strap. Tie cord in knot, leaving ends free about 3" beyond knot to form tassel. Center knot at bottom of bag and slipstitch along seam securing at sides.

7. Arrange one of each size starfish in an interlocking pattern on bag and slipstitch in place using upholstery thread.

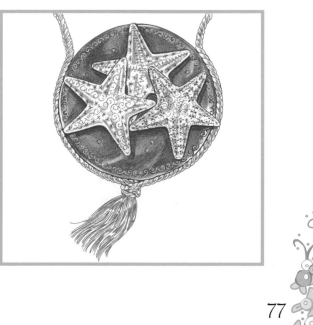

Dream Pillow

1. Cut 15" x 20" rectangles of pillow top fabric and batting. Baste together with right side of fabric facing up. Apply three rows of double needle topstitching diagonally from (1) upper left corner to lower right corner, (2) upper left side to center bottom, and (3) top left to right center, meandering slightly.

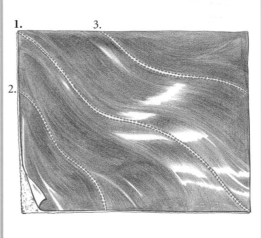

2. Topstitch between rows dividing empty spaces until entire pillow top is covered. (Note: Topstitching will alter dimensions of fabric unevenly.)

78

3. Apply fusible tricot interfacing to pillow back fabric and cut two 12½"x15" rectangles. Turn under ½", then ½" again to form hem on one 15" side of each rectangle. Machine stitch.

4. Pin backs to front, right sides together with backs overlapping in center. Place over pillow form and mark stitching line with air-soluble marker around outer edge to correspond to pillow form edges. (Note: You will have excess, uneven seam allowances on pillow top because of distortion from topstitching.)

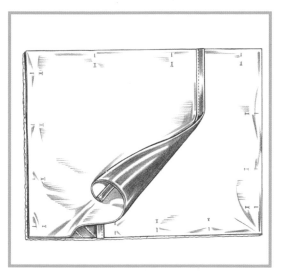

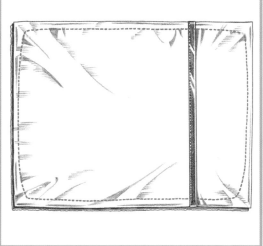

5. Stitch along marked lines, indenting slightly at corners to ensure good fit and proper shape. Trim seam to ½".

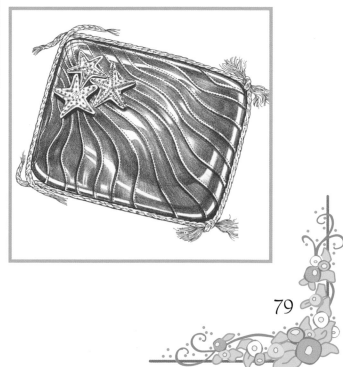

6. Turn right side out and insert pillow form. Cut heavy gold cording into 4 pieces, 10" longer than pillow measurements. Stitch invisibly to all four sides of pillow, leaving 5" of cord free on all corners. Tie ends in square knots, leaving free about 3" beyond knot to form tassel. Arrange starfish in interlocking pattern and slipstitch in place with upholstery or carpet thread.

MATERIALS:

Calla Lilies
(5 flowers, 6 leaves)

- ⅔ yd white velour or velveteen fabric
- ⅓ yd green moiré fabric
- ⅓ yd green satin fabric
- ¼ yd yellow velour fabric
- 1 yd yellow fringe
- 1 yd green stretch knit
- ⅔ yd polyester batting
- 6 vinyl-covered 3' garden stakes
- 15' of ½" diam. polybutylene pipe
- green rayon embroidery thread

Anthuriums
(5 flowers, 6 leaves)

- ⅔ yd red velour or velveteen fabric
- ⅓ yd green moiré fabric
- ⅓ yd green satin fabric
- ¼ yd yellow velour fabric
- ⅔ yd polyester batting
- 7 yds green ¼" velvet cording
- 25' roll vinyl-covered clothesline wire
- red rayon embroidery thread
- air-soluble marker
- glue gun
- wire cutters

80

Calla Lilies & Anthuriums

*T*he calla lilies are in bloom all year with these beautiful floral sculptures. The regal white blooms share many of the same patterns and techniques with the flamboyant tropical anthuriums. Add cool understated elegance or warm island color to your decor.

Instructions:

Calla Lilies

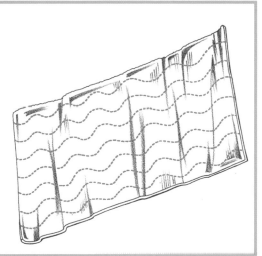

1. Cut a 9" x 18" rectangle of yellow velour. Using embroidery thread, apply decorative running zig zag in allover pattern.

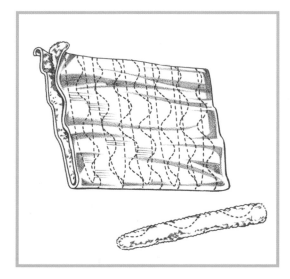

2. Fold stamen fabric in half, right sides together and trace stamen template five times leaving ½" between stitching lines. Stitch along lines, leaving open at lower edge. Cut apart, leaving ¼" seam allowances. Turn right side out.

TECHNIQUES:

Transferring patterns onto fabric, page 34
Interlocking pattern layout, page 35
Sewing, then cutting, page 39
Tips for turning, page 41
Topstitching and free-motion quilting, page 39
Decorative machine embroidery, page 47

MEASURING:

Tracing and measuring information is included within each flower instruction.

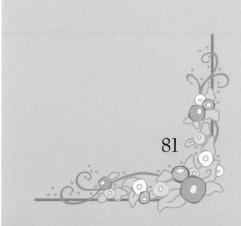

81

3. To make petals and leaves, place two layers of fabric, right sides together with batting underneath. Trace petal template five times and leaf template six times using interlocking pattern layout, leaving ½" between shapes. Stitch along outlines, leaving 1" opening at center bottom for turning. Cut apart, leaving ¼" seam allowances. Clip and trim. Turn.

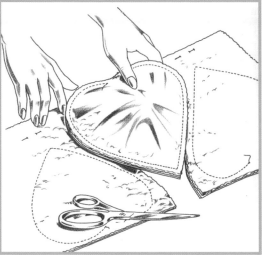

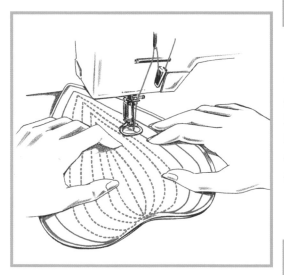

4. To make petals, turn under raw edges of opening at lower edge, and pin closed. Mark topstitching lines with air-soluble marker, or use free-motion stitching to create quilted pattern as shown. Stitch close to pinned lower edge.

5. Cut green stretch knit into 1¾" x 36" strips. Fold strips of stem fabric lengthwise, right sides together. Measure around pipe and garden stakes and mark appropriate stitching lines for snug fit. Stitch to form tubes leaving one end open. Trim seams to ¼".

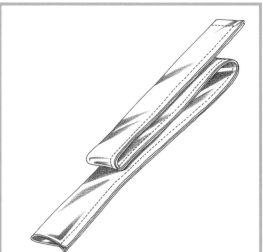

6. To turn stem, insert pipe into stitched end of tube and turn right side out, straightening seam along full length of pipe.

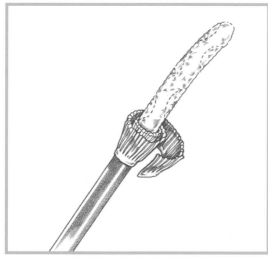

7. Turn raw edges of tubing into open end of pipe, insert open end of stamen into pipe and glue in place. Cut yellow fringe into five 7" pieces. Wrap fringe around stem several times, covering joint between stamen and stem. Glue to secure.

8. Wrap petal snugly around stamen and stem below fringe, overlapping lower edges approximately 1½" to form flower shape. Glue to secure.

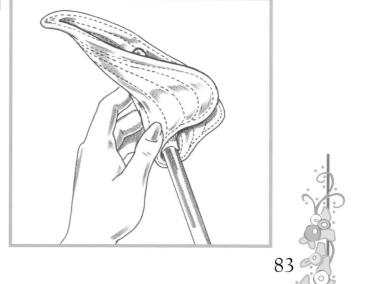

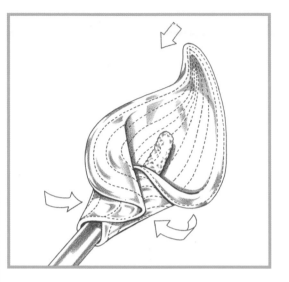

9. Fold back outer edges of petal to form cup-like shape so that fringe is visible.

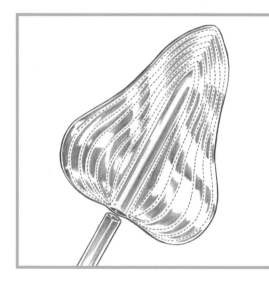

10. Mark and topstitch leaves, ensuring center channel is left open to insert the stem. To assemble, insert stem into center channel of leaf. Glue to secure.

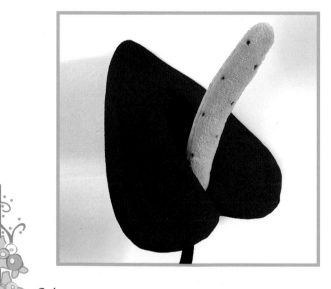

Anthurium

Follow steps 2-4 above using anthurium fabrics. Cut a 9" X 18" rectangle of yellow velour. Mark fabric with air-soluble marker at ½" intervals in alternating rows. To create machine french knots, lower feed dogs and set machine to narrow satin stitch with memory set for five repetitions. Engage pattern begin and end. Stitch as marked. Trim threads close to stitching.

84

11. Cut vinyl-covered wire into 11 pieces of varying lengths from 15" to 30". Bend one end of wire under ¼" and wrap with a small amount of batting. Insert wire fully into each stamen. Remove thin white cord from center of velvet cording and thread cording onto wire stems. Glue to secure where stamen meets stem.

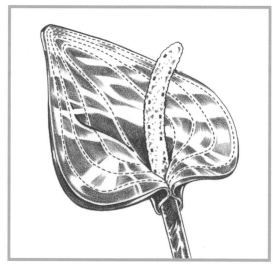

12. Apply glue to center of lower edge of petal. Wrap petal around stamen and pinch together to form flower. Allow glue to dry fully then flatten flower perpendicular to stamen.

13. Mark and topstitch leaves ensuring center channel is left open. Insert covered stems fully into center channel of leaves. Glue to secure. Bend leaves slightly outward with moiré side up.

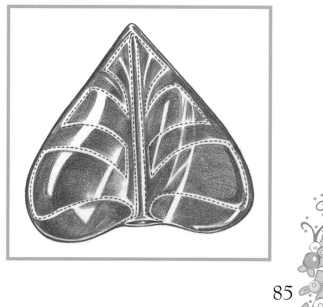

85

MATERIALS:

- 1 yd (or 10-12"x12" squares) cream suedecloth
- ½ yd (or 5-12"x12" squares) green suedecloth
- ½ yd (or 5-12"x12" squares) tan suedecloth
- 1-12"x12" square burgundy suedecloth
- 2 yds-3½" wide wire-edged tapestry ribbon
- 1 small piece gold metallic crinkle organza
- 3 yds light fusible web
- matching green rayon embroidery thread
- monofilament thread
- polyester fiberfill (small amount)
- 6" vinyl-covered clothesline wire
- 8 pieces florist wire
- green florist tape
- 2 dz 1" green-glass bugle beads
- 2 dz small round red wooden beads
- multi-colored metallic 16mm braid
- embroidery needle
- beading thread
- beading needle
- upholstery thread
- air-soluble marker
- glue gun

86

Magnolia

Sculpted from faux-suede with delicate hand-stitched beading and embellishment, this elegant magnolia blossom, bud and foliage evoke memories of fragrant southern gardens. They can be used as a holiday spray, an exotic centerpiece or arranged with candles and tapestry ribbon for a stunning mantle display.

Instructions:

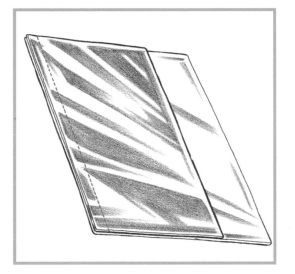

1. With right sides facing, stitch burgundy and tan pieces along one 12" side using ¼" seam allowance to create two-tone color block fabric.

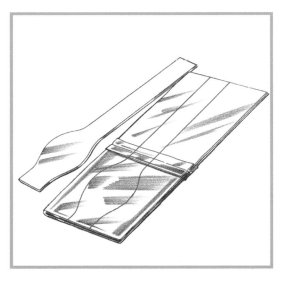

2. Open seams and fold fabric, right sides together, matching seams carefully. Aligning seam with mark, trace stem template using air-soluble marker.

TECHNIQUES:

Color blocking, page 35
Sewing, then cutting, page 39
Stuffing, pages 41-42
Tips for turning, page 41
Fusing fabrics together, page 35
Interlocking pattern layout, page 35
Hand embellishment, page 49
Wrapping, page 48
Gathering, page 40

MEASURING:

Cut one piece burgundy suede, 6"x12", and one piece tan suede, 9"x12".

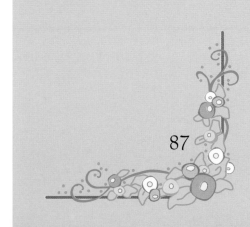

87

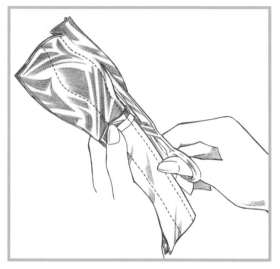

3. Stitch along marked lines leaving both ends open. Cut out leaving ¼" seam allowance. Sew across tan stem end to close.

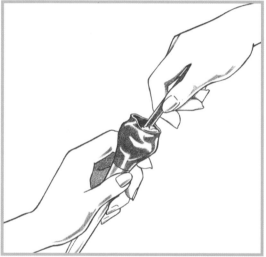

4. Use paint brush handle or point turner to turn stem right side out. Stuff lightly with polyester fiberfill. Bend one end of vinyl-covered wire under ¼" and wrap with a small amount of stuffing. Insert wire into stem and stuff firmly with fiberfill to widest part. Turn in raw edges to enclose stuffing and flatten upper end. Glue to secure.

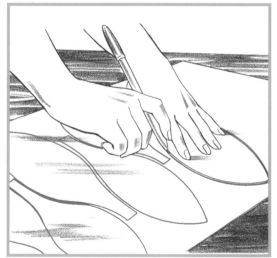

5. Following manufacturer's instructions, join 2 layers of cream suede cloth, right sides out, using fusible web. With air-soluble marker, using interlocking pattern layout, trace small petal template ten times, and larger petal template ten times to form ten pairs of petal pieces. Cut out carefully.

88

6. Thread machine with monofilament thread and set to narrow zig zag stitch. Align two petal pieces so that flat edges are touching side-by-side, matching ends carefully. Center under presser foot and stitch together. Repeat to make ten petals.

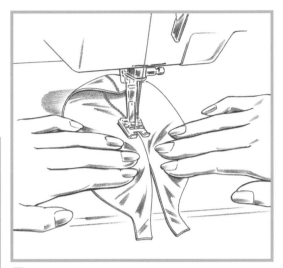

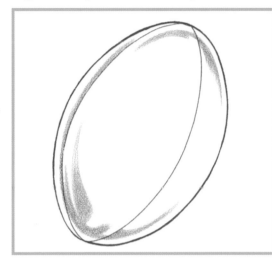

7. Trace base template four times on tan suede cloth. Cut out along traced lines. Sew together using ¼" seam allowance to form egg-like shape, leaving one end open. Turn, stuff lightly with fiberfill. Glue to close.

8. Cut one 6"x12" piece of organza. Sew short ends together to form tube. Run gathering stitch along top and bottom of tube.

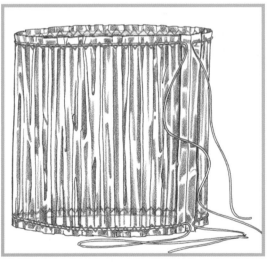

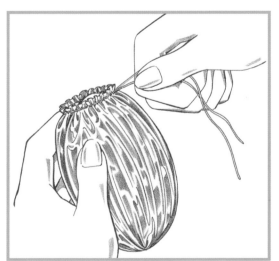

9. Pull gathering threads at one end very tightly and knot to secure. Turn right side out. Insert stuffed base and pull remaining gathering threads to enclose completely. Tie gathering threads securely.

89

10. Thread embroidery needle with metallic braid. Starting about ¾" from one end of base, make one row of long stitches, creating ½" loops around base. For second row, use interlocking stitches, to form fish-net-like web.

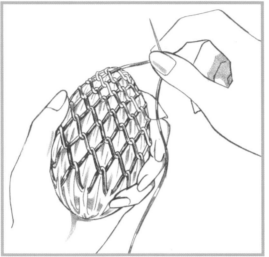

11. Cover entire base with stitches, gradually decreasing stitch size toward top of base, as illustrated.

12. Glue base to stem. Using beading needle and thread, attach bugle beads and round wooden beads around lower edge of base.

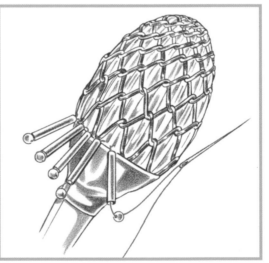

13. Glue three small and four large petals in place on stem, arranging them in overlapping layers.

14. Roll remaining large petal tightly, overlapping sides to form center of bud. Arrange remaining smaller petals on either side of large petal, overlapping to form tightly closed bud. Glue to secure. Bend florist wire in half lengthwise. Place at base end of bud and wrap with florist tape to create stem.

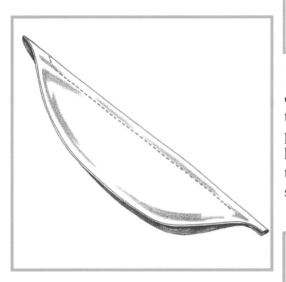

15. Fuse together tan and green suede cloth. Using interlocking pattern layout, trace on tan side, 5 of each size leaf templates (15 leaves). Cut out carefully. Fold leaves in half lengthwise with green sides together and stitch ¼" from fold to create stem channel.

16. Bend florist wire in half lengthwise. Insert ends into leaf channels. Open out leaves and bend slightly to sculpt. Wrap ends of leaves and wire with green florist tape. Arrange blossom, leaves and bud with tapestry ribbon to complete.

CHAPTER 9

Advanced Projects

Your creativity can soar to new heights when you master the techniques required to complete these advanced projects. Their scale and complexity offer challenges and exciting solutions to expand your artistic horizons from the earthly to the ethereal.

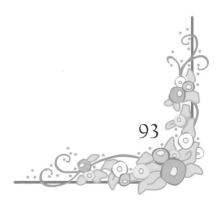

MATERIALS:

- 1 yd green suedecloth (artichoke)
- 1 yd dark green suedecloth (artichoke)
- ⅓ yd dark green suedecloth (acorn squash)
- ⅓ yd gold antique satin or moiré fabric (corn)
- ⅓ yd yarn-dyed organdy (corn)
- ⅓ yd each burgundy and green suedecloth (leaves)
- 1 yd khaki suedecloth (leaves, okra, butternut squash)
- ⅓ yd vanilla suedecloth (okra)
- variegated earth-toned rayon thread (corn)
- monofilament or matching thread
- metallic gold thread
- ⅔ yd Sashua trim, Glissengloss by Madeira (artichoke)
- 2 yds fusible web
- ⅓ yd fusible tricot interfacing
- perforated embroidery stabilizer
- 1 bag polyester fiberfill
- 25' of 28-gauge gold tone wire (corn)
- leather machine needle
- edgestitch foot
- walking foot with guide
- air-soluble marker
- glue gun

94

Autumn Harvest Vegetables

*T*he textures, tone and shapes of these unique soft sculpture vegetables are sure to become a treasured part of your autumn decor. Acorn and butternut squash, okra, artichoke, Indian corn and autumn leaves combine to make a delightful arrangement. Display them in a favorite basket or bowl, create a beautiful table spray, or attach them to a welcoming wreath.

Instructions:

Corn

TECHNIQUES:

Transferring patterns onto fabric, page 34
Sewing, then cutting page 39
Fusing fabrics together, page 35
Serged wire edge, page 48
Slash and turn, page 41
Stack and stitch, page 38
Tips for turning, page 41
Stuffing, pages 41-42

MEASURING:

Tracing and measuring information is included within each vegetable instruction.

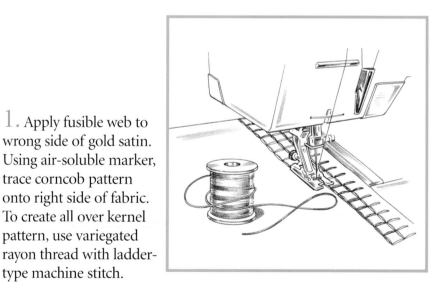

1. Apply fusible web to wrong side of gold satin. Using air-soluble marker, trace corncob pattern onto right side of fabric. To create all over kernel pattern, use variegated rayon thread with ladder-type machine stitch. Stitch one straight row down right side of corn cob piece, creating first row of kernels. Align second and subsequent rows of stitches to the left edge of previous line of stitching, using inside of right toe of presser foot as a guide. Continue sewing rows until entire corn cob surface is covered.

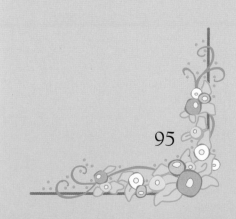

2. Cut out corn cob piece, leaving ¼" seam allowance. Stitch sides together leaving open at wide end to stuff. Stuff with polyester fiberfill to within ½" of open end. Fold in raw edges and glue to secure.

3. Cut organdy into four 3" strips. Using rayon thread, create corn husk texture by stitching several rows of straight stitches ¼" apart the entire length of strips.

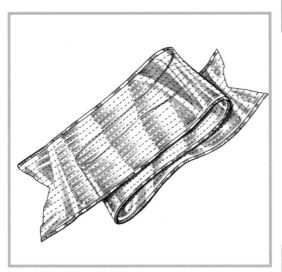

4. Attach cording foot to serger and adjust to rolled edge setting. Thread machine with rayon thread. Insert wire through foot for rolled edging. Serge edges of organdy around wire to create wire-edged ribbon husks. Cut into lengths of 18" to 24". Cut ends of ribbons in V shape and twist wire ends as shown.

5. Stack ribbons from longest to shortest, matching centers. Tie a loose knot at center to form stem.

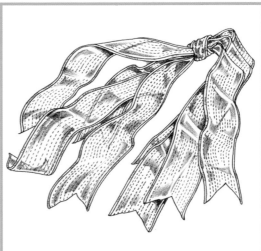

96

6. Glue to wide end of corn cob and shape around cob to form corn husk. Pull longest ribbons around pointed end of cob and twist together to simulate tassel. Twist and shape shorter ribbons around corn for naturally dried look.

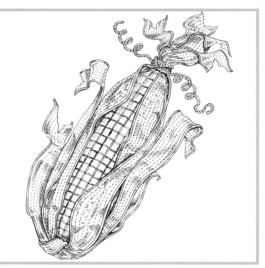

Okra

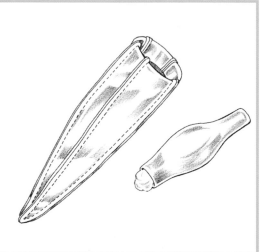

1. Using air-soluble marker, trace okra stem template on double layer of khaki suedecloth. Stitch around three sides leaving one end open to turn. Cut out leaving $\frac{1}{4}$" seam allowance. Turn and stuff with polyester fiberfill.

2. Apply fusible web to wrong side of khaki suedecloth. Fuse to vanilla suedecloth. Using air-soluble marker, trace okra template five times for each pod. Cut out along marked lines. Stitch together with vanilla sides facing using $\frac{1}{4}$" seam allowance. (Note: Seam allowances will face out to form ribs on pod.) Trim seam allowances carefully to $\frac{1}{8}$". Turn under upper edge $\frac{1}{4}$" and glue to secure. Insert stem into pod and glue.

97

Butternut Squash

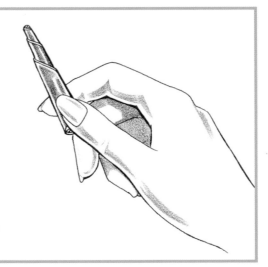

1. Cut a 2¼" x 2¼" square of khaki suedecloth. Twirl to form a twisted stem. Glue to secure.

2. Using air-soluble marker, and interlocking pattern layout, trace butternut squash template 5 times onto wrong side of khaki suedecloth, leaving ½" between shapes. Cut out leaving ¼" seam allowances. With right sides together, stitch squash pieces together leaving small opening at top. Stuff with fiberfill. Insert stem and glue to secure. Make one leaf following leaf instructions and glue to stem.

Artichoke

1. Using an air-soluble marker and interlocking pattern layout, trace artichoke base template on wrong side of green or dark green suedecloth four times for each artichoke, leaving ½" between shapes. Cut out leaving ¼" seam allowances.

2. With right sides together, stitch artichoke pieces together leaving small opening at top. Stuff with fiberfill. Stitch ends closed. Glue decorative Madeira thread around top of base to simulate thistle.

3. Fold remaining green suedecloth in half lengthwise, right sides out. Using air-soluble marker and interlocking pattern layout, trace artichoke leaf template thirteen times, leaving ½" between shapes. Stitch around marked lines. Cut out and trim seam allowances to ⅛". Match seams center front to center back. Shape to form three-dimensional leaf. Stitch across leaf slightly below center to secure. Fold each leaf at topstitching to form double leaf.

4. Glue leaves to artichoke base so that points meet at top of thistle. Form three layers of double leaves covering the base, overlapping and centering each between previous layer.

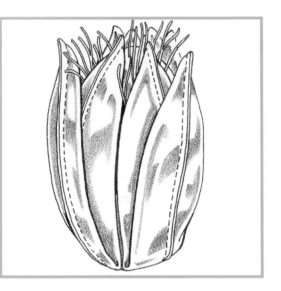

5. Fold suedecloth, right sides facing. Using air-soluble marker, trace artichoke stem template on double thickness. Stitch using $\frac{1}{4}$" seam allowances, leaving open at widest end to turn. Cut out, turn and stuff firmly to widest part of stem. Fold down remaining fabric to flatten and glue to secure. Glue to base.

Acorn Squash

1. Fold dark green suedecloth lengthwise, right sides together. Using air-soluble marker and interlocking pattern layout, trace acorn squash template five times, and stem template one time, leaving $\frac{1}{2}$" between shapes.

2. Stitch around stem leaving open at widest end to turn. Stitch completely around squash shapes. Cut out leaving $\frac{1}{4}$" seam allowances. Slit squash shapes as indicated on pattern to turn.

3. Stack turned shapes, matching edges and stitch through center.

100

4. Stuff each channel very firmly with polyester fiberfill. (Note: If stuffed firmly enough, it is not necessary to close slits.) Turn stem right side out and stuff upper half. Turn under edges and glue to stem end of squash.

5. To make wired thread chain tendrils, attach cording foot to serger and adjust to rolled edge setting. Thread with rayon thread. Insert wire through roll edge foot. Serge over wire.

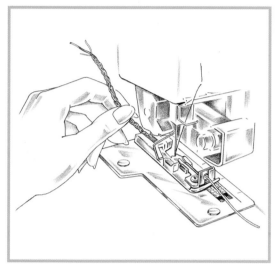

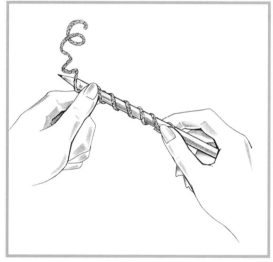

6. Wrap tendril around pencil to form spiral. Remove from pencil carefully.

7. Twist tendril around squash stem.

Khaki, Burgundy, and Green Leaves

1. Cut each fabric in half to create 6" strips. Apply fusible web to one strip of each color. Fuse fabrics together in various color combinations.

2. Using air-soluble marker, trace leaf templates nine times on fused fabrics. Cut out carefully. Mark folding/topstitching lines.

3. Fold along center line and stitch ¼" from fold. Fold diagonal lines and stitch ¼" from fold to form ribs. Stitch from center toward outer edge of leaves.

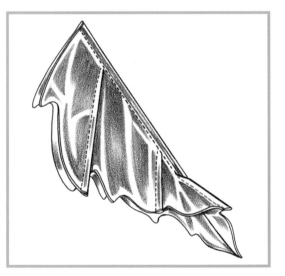

Arrange these versatile vegetables and leaves throughout the house creating an elegant and festive autumn decor. Here are but a few of the endless possibilities for their use:

Create a colorful and inviting interior door display by tying several ears of corn together at the base of the husks. Add extra husks and wired tendrils to make a full, bountiful-looking spray.

Fill miniature baskets with nuts intermingled with multi-colored sculpted leaves and tendrils. Positioned at each place setting you've added your own personal touch to your holiday table.

Design a beautiful fall wreath as a door decoration or centerpiece. Attach artichoke and okra pods near the center top of a grapevine wreath. Insert florist wire into channels of leaves and fill in around the vegetables. Finish with a wire-edged tapestry ribbon bow.

103

MATERIALS:

- 2 yds pale green moiré fabric (screen)
- 1 yd pink moiré fabric (tulips)
- ⅓ yd white satin fabric (daffodils)
- ⅓ yd yellow knit fabric
- 2 yds green knit fabric (leaves and stems)
- ⅔ yd dark green knit fabric
- ⅓ yd light blue moiré fabric (iris)
- ⅓ yd sky blue moiré fabric
- 4½ yds green moiré fabric (strap and tulip leaves)
- 4½ yds 17"-fusible web
- ⅔ yd fusible tricot interfacing
- 45" x 60" polyester batting
- 2 yds yellow rayon cording (rattail)
- 1-30" x 40" foam core board
- 19-24" pieces florist wire
- 18-20" plastic balloon straws
- matching thread
- glue gun
- air-soluble marker
- utility knife
  - metal ruler

104

Fireplace Screen

*W*hether you live in the country or the
city, this fireplace screen brings a touch of spring gardens
indoors. Colorful flowers and richly textured foliage
of perennial favorites bloom from a three-paneled garden
wall. The bas-relief and fully dimensional flowers
are a welcome addition to your hearth
to announce the arrival of spring.

Instructions:

Daffodil

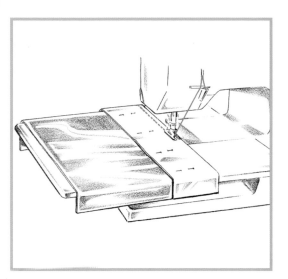

1. Cut 4½" x 45" strip of yellow knit and 20" x 45" strip of green knit. Align edges and pin, right sides together. Stitch using ¼" seam allowance. Press seam open.

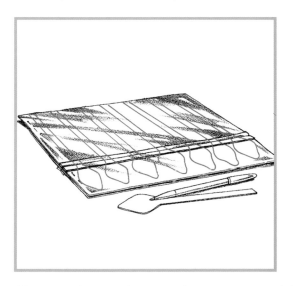

2. Fold in half, right sides together, matching seams carefully. Using air-soluble marker, trace daffodil center/stem template seven times, aligning mark on template with seam, leaving ½" between shapes.

TECHNIQUES:

Color blocking, page 35
Topstitching and free-motion quilting, page 39
Tips for turning, page 41
Pressing, page 42
Stuffing, pages 41-42
Sewing, then cutting, page 39
Interlocking pattern layout, page 35
Fusing fabrics together, page 35
Slash and turn, page 41
Fusing after sewing, page 43

MEASURING:

Tracing and measuring information is included within each flower instruction.

105

3. Stitch along marked lines leaving open at stem end. Cut out leaving ¼" seam allowances. Turn right side out.

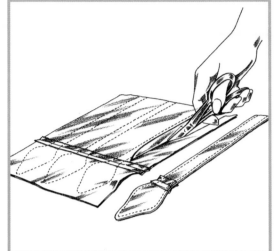

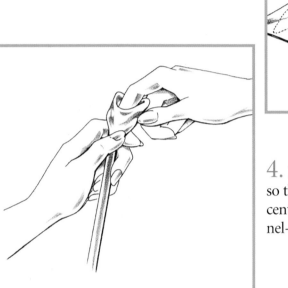

4. Insert balloon straws into green stems so that straw extends at least 1" into yellow center. Turn in bulbous end to create funnel-shaped cup-like center.

5. Apply fusible tricot interfacing to white satin. Fold fabric in half crosswise and with air-soluble marker, trace daffodil petal template seven times. Stitch completely around each shape, pivoting at points. Cut out leaving ¼" seam allowances. Trim and clip points. Make a small X-shaped slit through both layers of each flower and turn right side out, using paint brush handle to open petals fully. Press. Topstitch each petal as shown. Clip topstitching threads to re-open slit.

6. Insert green stem through slit and push daffodil petals beyond end of balloon straw. Remaining yellow cup forms center of daffodil.

Daffodil / Iris Leaf

7. Cut two 1⅔ yds pieces of green moiré. Place right sides together. Using air-soluble marker and interlocking pattern layout, trace large strap leaf template nine imes, and small strap leaf template ten times, leaving ½" between shapes. Stitch, leaving open at bottom edge. Cut out, leaving ¼" seam allowance. Match seams in center, press leaves.

8. Trace templates onto backing paper of fusible web and cut out one piece for each leaf, slightly smaller than leaf size. Following manufacturer's instructions, apply fusible web to one side of each leaf.

9. Remove backing paper from fusible web and turn leaf right side out using paint brush handle. Insert florist wire into center of each leaf along center seam line. Press each leaf again to fuse layers together and secure wire.

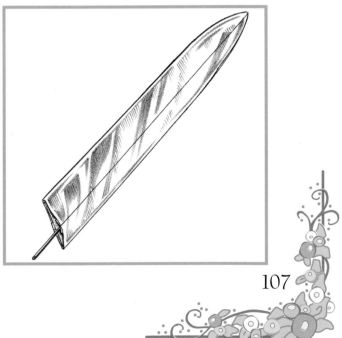

107

Tulip

10. Apply fusible tricot interfacing to green moiré fabric. Place green knit and moiré, right sides together, batting underneath. Using interlocking pattern layout, trace large tulip leaf template fifteen times and small tulip leaf template twelve times, leaving ½" between shapes. Stitch, leaving open at lower edge. Cut out leaving ¼" seam allowances. Trim points and turn. Turn raw edges to inside and press.

11. Topstitch two rows ¼" apart through center of each leaf, beginning at lower edge, pivoting at point. Fold large leaves lengthwise, knit inside. Glue.

12. Apply fusible tricot interfacing to pink moiré. Fold fabric, right sides together. Using interlocking pattern layout, trace tulip petal template 23 times, leaving ½" between shapes. Stitch leaving ½" open on one side to turn. Cut out leaving ¼" seam allowances. Trim points. Cut eight pieces in half crosswise. Turn and press all leaves, matching seams in center of petal.

13. Fold in half diagonally with open seam to inside. (Note: Angle may be varied for buds or fully opened blooms.) Glue half petals to folded petals, centering to form tulip blooms. Attach to stems.

Iris

14. To make iris stems, cut 1¾" strips of dark green knit. Fold lengthwise right sides together and stitch ⅜" from fold, leaving ends open. Trim seams to ¼". Cut into nine pieces of varying lengths of 12" to 20". Stitch across one end of each piece. Place balloon straw into stitched end and turn right side out over balloon straw. Glue to secure at open end.

15. Cut nine 5" pieces of yellow rattail trim. Tie a knot in center of each piece. Pull small center cord to fray at both ends.

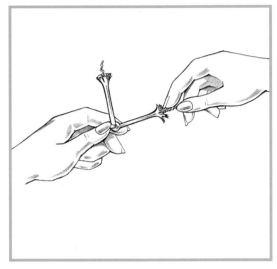

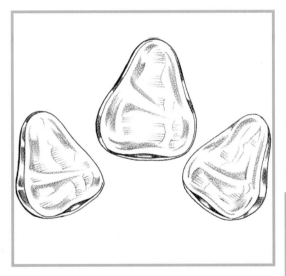

16. Place light blue moiré and sky blue moiré, right sides together with batting underneath. Using air-soluble marker and Interlocking pattern layout, trace large iris petal template nine times, and small iris petal template eighteen times, leaving ½" between shapes. Stitch leaving lower edge open to turn. Cut out leaving ¼" seam allowances. Trim points and turn.

17. Glue knot of stamen to end of stem as shown. Fold large iris petal around stem. Pinching lower edges together, glue to secure.

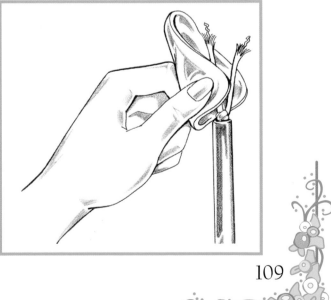

109

18. Apply a small amount of glue to center of each small iris petal and pinch together. Attach two small petals to upper edge of stem just under large petal.

Fireplace screen

19. Using utility knife and metal ruler, measure and cut foam core board into three panels. Cut two 10" x 30" pieces and one 20" x 30" piece.

20. Fold light green moiré fabric, right sides together with moiré running vertically. Place foam core panels on fabric leaving ¼" between panels. Using air-soluble marker, trace around outer edges of panels. Stitch around three sides, leaving open one long side. Cut away excess fabric leaving ½" seam allowance. Leave 1" on lower edge for hem. Trim corners, turn right side out. Press.

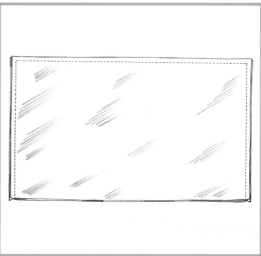

21. Insert foam core panels, large board in center and smaller panels on either side. Carefully pin between panels. Using air-soluble marker, mark topstitching lines.

22. Remove panels and turn in raw edges to form 1" hem. Press. Pin lower edges together carefully and topstitch along marked lines. Reinsert panels and slipstitch closed across bottom edge.

23. Arrange leaves and flowers on panels as shown, beginning with large strap leaves and tallest flowers. Glue to secure. Finish with small flat tulip leaves along lower edge.

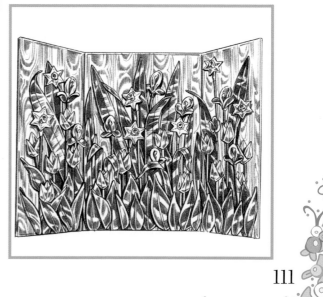

MATERIALS:

- 1⅓ yd ivory satin fabric
- 3½ yds-¼" flat gold braid
- 1 yd metallic gold crinkle organza
- 12"x6" polyester batting
- ⅓ yd muslin
- 1-11"x14" plastic canvas
- polyester fiberfill
- 1⅓ yds fusible tricot interfacing
- ⅓ yd-¼" elastic cord
- metallic gold embroidery thread
- ⅓ yd wired metallic gold braid (halo)
- porcelain doll head and arms
- ivory thread
- ¼ yd vinyl-covered clothesline wire
- braiding foot
- free-motion quilting foot
- glue gun
- air-soluble marker

Angel Treetopper

Reminiscent of a Renaissance painting, this beautiful treetop angel is sure to become a treasured heirloom for seasonal celebrations. Her delicate features are enhanced by opulent robes, richly embellished with gold cords, metallic embroidery, and trapunto stitching. She can also be used as a festive centerpiece or a heavenly addition to your collection.

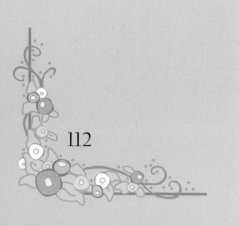

Instructions:

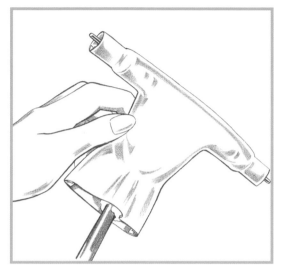

1. Stitch muslin along traced lines leaving open at lower edge of body and ends of arms. Cut out leaving ¼" seam allowances. Clip corners and turn. Insert vinyl-covered wire through sleeves. Lightly stuff upper body to narrowest part of waist with polyester fiberfill, using paint brush handle to distribute fiberfill evenly.

2. Place angel body over top of cone and pull down snugly. Glue to secure. Glue porcelain arms to vinyl-covered wires carefully, positioning thumbs upward. Turn under raw edges of sleeves; glue to arms. Center doll head between shoulders and glue in place.

TECHNIQUES:

Sewing, then cutting, page 39
Stuffing, pages 41-42
Tips for turning, page 41
Slash and turn, page 41
Decorative machine embroidery, page 47
Hand embellishment, page 49
Fusing fabrics together, page 35
Gathering, page 40
Creating an armature, page 138
Transferring patterns onto fabric, page 34
Cords, trims, and tassels, page 46

MEASURING:

Trace body template onto double layer of muslin.

Form cone from plastic canvas, overlapping corners. Glue to secure. Trim lower edge of plastic canvas so that cone will stand evenly.

113

3. Drape satin fabric over cone. Smooth and pin in place. Trim excess fabric leaving ½" seam allowance on back seam and 3½" extending below cone. Mark seam and remove from cone. With right sides together, stitch seam, leaving open 5" on top. Press seam open. Turn under upper edge ¼" and machine hem. Press under ¼" on lower edge. Turn up pressed edge ½" to form elastic casing. Stitch, leaving 1" open to insert elastic. Place skirt on cone. Whipstitch back seam. Thread elastic through casing, pull to fit and tie ends. Trim elastic and slipstitch casing closed.

4. Apply fusible tricot interfacing to ½ yd ivory satin. Using air-soluble marker, trace skirt panel template eight times onto right side of satin. Cut along traced lines.

5. With right sides together, pin panels so outside edge of one panel joins inside edge of next panel, matching inside tip to notch on outer edge. Baste ¼" from edge leaving back seam open.

6. Stitch along basting lines. Clip curves, pressing seams toward outside curve. Turn skirt panel template in opposite direction; trace eight times on unfused satin for skirt lining. Assemble lining panels as for skirt.

7. Apply decorative stitching using pre-programmed flower motifs and gold metallic thread. Stitch back seam leaving upper 5" open.

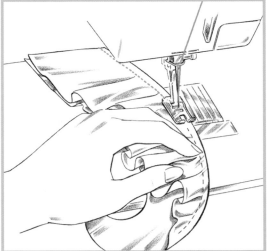

114

8. Using a braiding foot, couch braid over each seam. Backstitch at both ends to secure.

9. Pin lining to skirt, right sides together matching seams carefully. Stitch around lower scalloped edge of skirt ½" from edge. Trim to ¼", clip curves, turn and press. Pin lining to skirt around open back seam, folding in raw edges. Stitch close to edge to join.

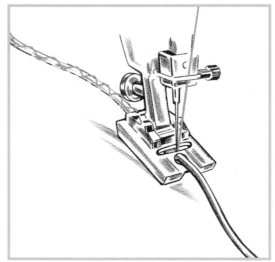

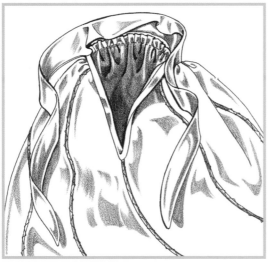

10. Measure waist of doll. Gather skirt to fit, about 7". Cut 30" x 2" strip of ivory satin for sash. Fold lengthwise, right sides together. Stitch ¼" from edge diagonally across both ends and down sides, leaving 7" open in center for waistband. Press under remaining seam allowance along one edge. Pin waistband to skirt, right sides together, adjusting gathers to fit. Stitch. Whipstitch remaining edge.

11. Put skirt on angel. Cross sash extensions in back and wrap across shoulders to front, crossing again to form bodice as illustrated. Glue to secure, leaving extensions free.

12. Cut 12" x 12" squarc of organza. Cut 6" x 12" piece of batting. Fold organza in half with batting underneath. Using air-soluble marker, trace wing template. Stitch completely around outline. Cut out leaving ¼" seam allowance. Clip points, trim curves and trim batting close to stitching. Make 2" vertical slash in center of wings through one layer of organza. Turn right side out. Whipstitch slit closed. Attach free-motion quilting foot. Beginning at upper edge of wings create all over free-motion scallop pattern, as illustrated.

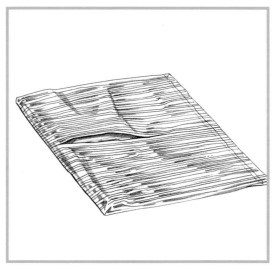

13. Cut 24" x 30" rectangle of organza. Fold in half along long edge and stitch up 6" with 1/4" seam. Turn right side out. Center seam and stitch across open short ends with 1/4" seam.

14. At open end of tube, roll back 2", then 2" again to create cuff.

15. To place stole on angel, slip cuff over head and around waist as shown.

16. Draw stole up under arms and flip back over head draping over shoulders, adjusting cuff as necessary to cover sleeves. Tuck sash ends under stole.

17. Twist together ends of wired gold braid, leaving 3" loop to form halo. Shape into circle.

18. To attach halo, place twisted wire trim at center back of shoulders under stole. Glue to secure, adjusting halo as necessary over angel's head.

19. Center wings between shoulders with wing seam to angel back. Stitch invisibly to body. Adjust stole cuff around wings.

117

MATERIALS:

- 2' x 2' piece of plywood
- 6' of 1" PVC pipe
- 1 flange fitting for PVC pipe
- 1 tomato cage
- large U-shaped staple
- duct tape
- 22' of ½" poly pipe
- 3' of 1" poly pipe
- 3' of 1" foam pipe insulation
- 4' of 4" plastic dryer duct
- 1 yd camel stretch velour (roots)
- 1⅔ yds brown foam-backed fleece fabric (trunk)
- 1 yd green stretch velour (upper trunk and stem wrapping)
- 3 yds green moiré fabric (leaves)
- 3 yds green foam-backed fleece (leaves)
- 1 yd brown knit fabric (coconuts)
- 1 bag polyester fiberfill
- 3 yds polyester batting
- 3 yds 60" fusible tricot interfacing
  - soft sculpture needle
  - upholstery thread
  - green and brown rayon thread
  - glue gun

118

Tropical Palm Tree

$\mathcal{Y}$ou can almost feel the cool island breezes flowing through the leaves of this full size palm tree complete with coconuts. A stunning focal point for any casual decor, this project can bring the whole family together for some creative fun! Our tree measures approximately 7 feet tall from roots to tip, and can easily be adapted for smaller spaces.

Instructions:

1. To make armature, cut 18" plywood circle. Attach flange fitting in center. Insert PVC pipe into flange. Center tomato cage over pipe and secure to plywood base with large U-shaped staples. Use duct tape to secure loose upper wires of tomato cage to PVC pipe.

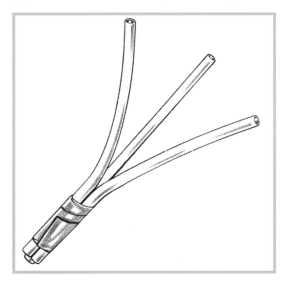

2. Tape three 18" pieces of poly pipe at one end with duct tape. Bend other ends outward to form central stem.

TECHNIQUES:

Transferring patterns onto fabric, page 34
Sewing, then cutting, page 39
Tips for turning, page 41
Interlocking pattern layout, page 35
Stuffing, pages 41-42
Wrapping, page 48
Circular stitching, page 38
Stack and stitch, page 38
Topstitching and free-motion quilting, page 39
Creating an armature, page 138

MEASURING:

Cut three 18" lengths of ½" poly pipe. Cut six 3' lengths of ½" poly pipe and three 1' lengths of 1" poly pipe. Cut three 1' lengths of foam pipe insulation.

Apply fusible tricot interfacing to wrong side of moiré.

119

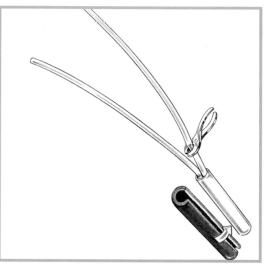

3. Insert two 3' pieces of ½" pipe into each 1" piece of poly pipe to a depth of at least 6", crimping smaller pipe as necessary with pliers to insert. Place foam pipe insulation over 1" pipes to thicken main stems.

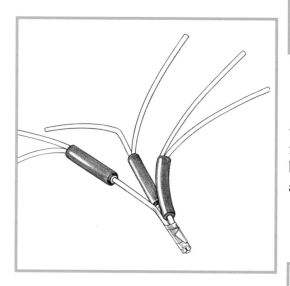

4. Insert each of the Y-shaped pipe configurations over the central stems to form branches which will hold palm leaves. Put aside for final assembly.

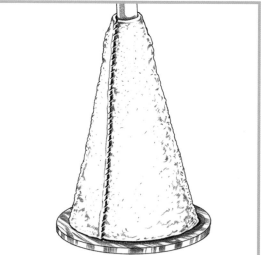

5. Drape a layer of polyester batting around tomato cage, pinning to fit. Trim away excess seam allowance. Using soft sculpture needle and upholstery thread, whipstitch cut edges together.

120

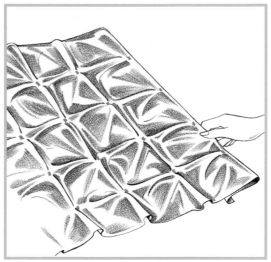

6. Create allover texture on trunk fabric, with air-soluble marker, marking in checker-board pattern, at 4" intervals. Using machine pre-programmed bartack function, fold fabric along marks and stitch ¼" from fold to create tucks.

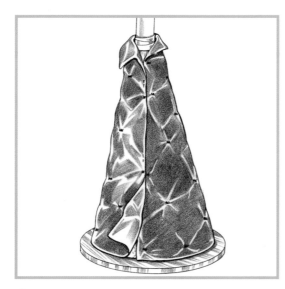

7. Drape tucked fabric around tomato cage. Pin to fit adjusting slightly near top to shape. Cut away excess fabric, leaving ½" seam allowance. Using air-soluble marker, mark seam lines. Remove from armature and machine stitch side seam. Turn right side out, slip over armature and adjust to fit. Bring upper ends together around PVC pipe at top of cage and tape in place.

8. Place two layers of camel velour right sides together. Using air-soluble marker, trace template onto fabric in interlocking pattern layout as shown, leaving at least ½" between shapes.

9. Stitch along traced lines. Cut apart leaving 1/4" seam allowances. Turn using point turner or paint brush handle. Stuff lightly with polyester fiberfill.

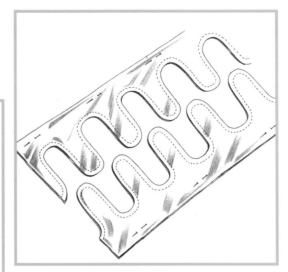

10. Stitch along open edges to close. Trim close to stitching. Use glue gun to attach roots to underside of tree trunk.

11. Cut three strips of green velour fabric, 2" X width of fabric. Serge one edge with coordinating decorative rayon thread. Beginning at center of Y, wrap velour around stem so that serged edge is visible, covering stem completely. Glue lower edge to secure.

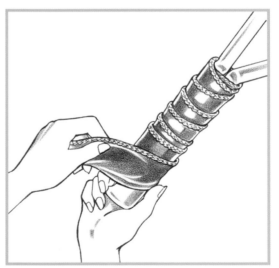

12. Measure green velour fabric so that it fits snugly around 4" dryer duct. Stitch together 4' length of velour to form tube.

13. Insert dryer duct into tube and pull to extend. Tuck ends of velour inside. Place covered duct over PVC pipe so that it covers taped edge of lower tree trunk. Whipstitch in place.

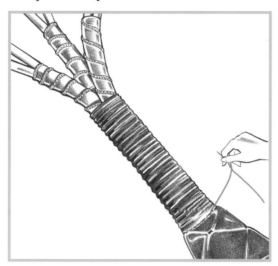

14. Insert central stem into upper trunk. Pull duct up over lower edge and tack in several places on each of the three central stems.

15. Place single layer of moiré and green fleece fabric right sides together. Trace leaf template six times. Stitch leaving open at blunt end. Trim seams, clip points and slit to inner points. Turn and press.

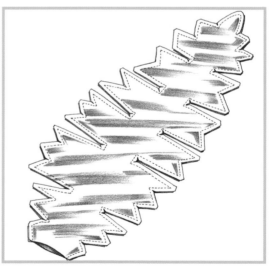

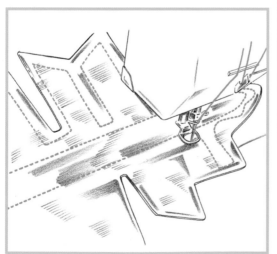

16. Using air-soluble marker, mark top-stitching channel on right side. Topstitch leaves along channel markings leaving open along blunt end for insertion of stem.

17. Slide leaves over stems and tack blunt end of leaf to wrapped stem ends with upholstery or quilting thread.

18. Follow same procedure as cacti, set circular embroidery attachment to 6" and stitch right sides together, double layers of brown knit fabric. For each coconut, make five sewn circles leaving open on one end. Turn right side out and stack five segments carefully. Stitch though center of all segments. Stuff lightly with fiberfill.

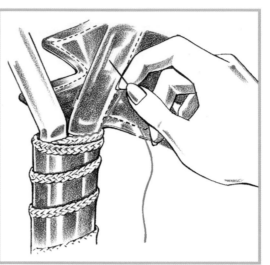

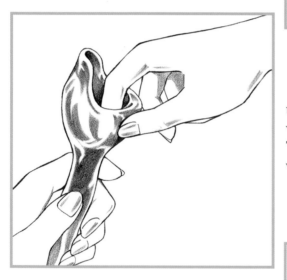

19. Trace coconut stem template three times onto double thickness of green velour fabric. Stitch leaving ends open. Trim and turn right side out. Turn in at widest end to form funnel shaped pieces.

20. Glue funnel-shaped ends of stems over open ends of coconuts.

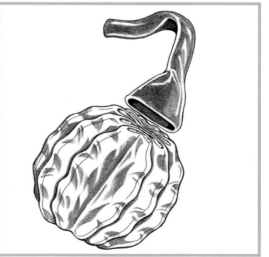

124

21. Bring three stems together and glue at raw ends.

22. Stitch two 3" circles of green stretch velour fabric, right sides together, leaving open ⅓ of each circle. Turn right side out, folding under raw edges. Slip over ends of coconut stems. Glue to secure.

23. Arrange coconuts between three main stems extending over upper trunk.

CHAPTER 10

Designing Your Own Projects

One of the most fascinating aspects of soft sculpture is that even the most familiar everyday object becomes artistically significant when recreated in fabric and thread. The infinite combinations of pattern, color and texture, coupled with the ability of fabric to conform to any shape, make it quite a versatile medium! Once you have completed the projects in this book, you might want to try your hand at designing your own.

127

How to See Like an Artist

To see like an artist you must learn to focus your attention on the elements of line, shape, form and space, value, texture, and color.

Creating your own original soft sculpture designs will become a fascinating preoccupation once you begin to see the world around you with the "new eyes" of a trained observer. By learning to recognize and appreciate the elements of design in everyday objects, both natural and manufactured, you can enhance your visual and sensory perception.

Line

Line defines the boundary around a shape, indicates a structural joint where two forms join, or it can be purely decorative as in a surface pattern. Converging lines simulate depth or perspective, vertical lines indicate thrust and power, horizontal lines seem restful, while diagonal lines indicate movement and create tension. Lines are straight or curved, thick or thin, solid or broken (broken lines are actually a series of short lines, but our minds tend to connect the

spaces between them so that we see a continuous "broken" line). In soft sculpting, seam lines, fold lines and topstitching lines can be placed strategically to give form or to create pattern or texture. Cording or piping can emphasize a line used as a boundary between shapes. Tucks, folds or pleats can look like a series of lines when used to create surface texture.

128

Shape

Shape refers to a two-dimensional area defined by a common element such as color, value or texture. Shapes are categorized as organic, which are freeform shapes such as those found in nature, and geometric or manufactured shapes, such as circles, squares, triangles, and so on. Upon close observation, many natural patterns and textures are geometric or orderly arrangements of shapes—fish scales, honeycombs, flower petal arrangements, etc. Designers of soft sculpture often begin to study an idea by thinking about how the shapes will fit together.

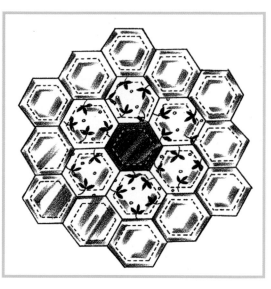

Form/Space

Forms are shapes seen in three dimensions. For instance, if a basic two-dimensional square were expanded to three dimensions it would become a cube. A circle might become a sphere (or perhaps a cylinder) and a triangle might become a pyramid or a cone. Like shapes, forms can be organic (natural) or geometric (manufactured) and when used together should relate to one another within the whole composition.

Space refers to the area surrounding a form. Sometimes the empty spaces between forms are interesting in and of themselves. For instance, imagine a flock of birds flying in formation—the space between the birds provides the contrast that allows you to see the pattern of the formation. In designing

129

soft sculpture it is important to consider the relationships between the forms and their environment.

Value

Value is the amount of light reflected from a surface. This can refer to the inherent amount of light or dark in a certain hue, or to the way it appears as a result of the surface texture. For instance, a glossy or shiny surface reflects much more light than a rough textured surface of the same hue.

Contrasts in value can be used to simulate three-dimensional forms because of the way the human eye translates light and dark into light and shadow. This phenomenon is often exploited in the design of quilt patterns which appear to be dimensional, and is the basis for realistic paintings in which depth is created totally by the indication of light and shadow. Use highly contrasting values of the same color to simulate shadow and exaggerate spatial relationships.

Texture

Texture is the way a surface feels or appears to feel. The very word "textile" evokes reference to the tactile sense. Using fabrics with contrasting textures provides surface interest which draws the observer into the work and stimulates the tactile sense.

130

Nature provides an encyclopedia of textures which serve various functions. Consider the smooth lining of a seed pod which cradles a delicate life-giving seed. Contrast it with the rough, prickly protective outer covering of that same seed.

Observing natural textures and translating them into fabric statements is central to a fiber artist's work. The creation of texture through surface embellishment is discussed in detail in the chapter entitled "Finishing Touches."

Color

Color is perhaps the most powerful and dynamic element of our visual perception and is probably the one which we notice first. The element of color is so powerful that it can cause emotional and even physical responses. Combinations of colors can create harmony or disharmony, agitation or restfulness, tension or calm. Nature provides an astonishing array of color combinations from which to glean inspiration. Begin by studying the combinations of colors within a single wildflower or a tiny insect, or notice the way an overcast day changes your color perception.

Color is defined by three characteristics:

Hue is that quality which allows us to differentiate between blue, red, yellow, etc. The human eye can detect even slight variations in hue (as you know if you've ever tried to match a fabric color exactly!).

131

Intensity refers to purity of hue or color saturation. It distinguishes a bright or vivid color from a muted tone, a tint or a shade.

Value is the amount of light reflected from a color. It can be measured by comparing the color to a gray scale which ranges from white to black. Becoming aware of the inherent value of a color will help create interesting contrasts in your selection of fabrics.

Since color is a function of light, it changes depending on the kind of light in which it is seen (natural daylight, incandescent or florescent). Furthermore, colors relate and react to one another so that when used in various combinations they may appear to change. Color theorists have devised various systems for organizing colors in order to understand and illustrate the relationships between them. One of the best and most universally accepted is a color wheel. It is an invaluable tool for the study and selection of colors and color combinations.

How to Generate Ideas

Now that you are seeing with artist's eyes, you can start exploring your world with that natural curiosity you had as a child when everything you encountered was new and exciting. You'll begin to notice the beautiful patterns of veins on a leaf, the way kernels of corn fit onto the cob, the texture of a coconut shell, the intricate combinations of colors on a butterfly wing—the list goes on forever.

132

To help you get inspired, listed below are just a few of the dozens of ideas for subjects which would translate beautifully into the medium of soft sculpture. You will quickly see that the possibilities are virtually unlimited. Just tune up your visual perception, unleash your imagination, and let it flow!

Plants

Trees, Houseplants, Cacti, Vines, Herbs, Wildflowers

Animals

Farm Animals, Pets, Zoo Animals, Jungle Animals, Teddy Bears, Birds, Fish, Snakes, Frogs, Turtles, Undersea Creatures, Insects, Fantasy Creatures, Dinosaurs

Food for Thought

Vegetables, Fruits, Nuts, Berries, Hot Dog, Hamburger, Taco, Pie, Cake, Muffin, Cookie, Tart, Sundae

Vehicles

Train, Airplane, Boat, Automobile, Truck, Spaceship, Hot Air Balloon, School Bus, Firetruck

People (dolls)

Historical figures, Literary figures, International dolls, Character dolls, Babies, Sports figures, Circus clowns, Dolls representing occupations (Doctor, Pilot, Nurse), Dolls representing celebrations (Weddings, Graduation, Holidays)

Furniture and appliances

Telephone, Toaster, Alarm Clock, TV, Radio, Book, Teapot, Sofa, Chair, Bed

Buildings

House, Church, Schoolhouse, Victorian Mansion, Castle, Skyscraper, Igloo, Tepee, Hut, Manger, Barn, Birdhouse

133

Looking at All the Angles

In order to translate ideas into soft sculpture patterns it is necessary to think about how the finished object will be seen from all directions. Once you've chosen a subject, think about the general characteristics first and the specific details will come later.

Begin in your mind's eye by imagining your finished piece as though you are standing directly in front of it. Use the questions below to clarify the image.

1. Is there one dominant shape or is it made up of several shapes joined together? How do those shapes relate to one another?

2. What do those shapes remind you of? Are they similar to basic geometric forms such as spheres, cubes, cylinders, pyramids or cones? Perhaps they are more organic (natural) and are shaped like leaves, fingers, branches, sea shells, and so on.

3. Think about the relationship of the height to the width. Is the overall piece wider than it is tall? Is it broader at the top or the bottom?

Now, using a pencil and paper draw a rough outline sketch of the overall shape or shapes that make up the piece as seen from directly in front.

Now, imagine that you are walking around to the back side of the piece. What does it look like from this side? How does it differ from the front? How is it similar to the front? Now sketch what the back side looks like.

134

Remember, this is just research and these rough sketches will never be seen by anyone else. The purpose of this exercise is strictly to put the idea into your mind. Repeat the same steps for the left and right sides, top (overhead view), and bottom.

Once you have a general idea of the shapes and how they relate to one another, you can begin to think about translating your two-dimensional drawings into three dimensions by creating patterns for them.

Soft sculpture differs from fashion sewing in that there is no "right or wrong" way to fit things together. You can design your pattern pieces very carefully and concisely or you can nip and tuck at will and allow the process of design to become part of your overall design. There is a certain freedom in that knowledge which releases your creativity so that you are free to experiment. Two excellent pattern making methods are described below:

Building a paper model

In designing an item to be stuffed, one very effective way to create soft sculpture patterns is to create a paper model. Once the model is constructed from paper, the main shapes and forms are then disassembled and adjusted until they can be flattened out into flat paper patterns.

It's a good idea to make the model about the same size you want the finished piece. However, for very large projects you might work small first, then enlarge to scale once the model is complete.

135

For this exercise you will need some heavy paper (brown paper grocery bags or old manilla folders are excellent), masking tape and scissors.

Using your rough sketches as a guide, cut and fold a piece of paper into a basic three-dimensional geometric form (cone, cylinder, pyramid, cube, etc.) which closely approximates the largest shape in your sketches, taping where necessary to hold the form together. Looking at the drawings again, add secondary shapes, trimming them as necessary and taping them into place on the main form. The parts won't fit together perfectly, but add tape wherever you need it to bridge any gaps and to hold things together.

You can overlap edges to take in a piece, add strips as necessary to enlarge, clip out darts, fold small pleats to simulate gathers or pinch in a small tuck. Just be careful to tape everything together well.

Once your model is all taped together, the next task is to translate it into pattern pieces by flattening it out. Instead of untaping the joints, use your scissors to separate each shape from the others, being careful to mark crucial

136

connecting points with colored markers or letters so that you can reconstruct the model as necessary. Then clip each shape at various points until it will lie flat. Your goal is to simplify the construction as much as possible while maintaining the integrity of the shapes.

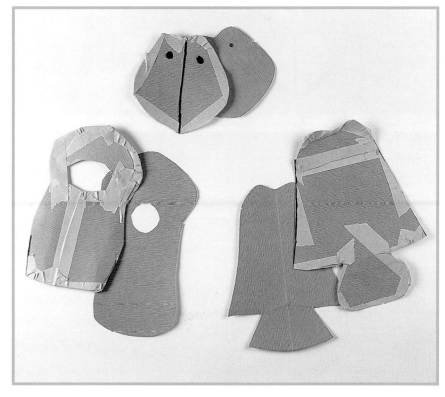

When you recreate these forms in fabric they will be much more fluid and flexible. Additionally, you will be able to manipulate the fabric somewhat in the stuffing process. The key to success is to experiment, adjust the shape of a dart so that it curves slightly or lengthen or shorten it to smooth out a shape. Use your model pattern as a starting point and trace its outline onto pattern paper. You can then make whatever adjustments you need to onto the second or third generation pattern, preserving your original model pattern as a reference.

You can fine tune your patterns using paper, but the real test will come when you make up a fabric sample. Use fabrics similar in weight and content to the ones you will be using for the final piece. Some designers like to stuff the first

fabric version inside out so that adjustments can be marked directly onto the seam lines.

Creating an armature

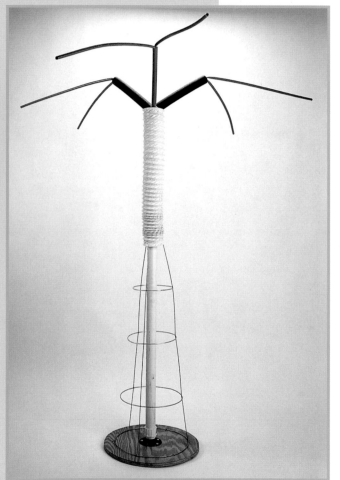

For very large items which require an armature or some sort of internal support, you must start with the "skeleton" and work your way out.

Using your drawings as a guide, create the armature from "found objects," PVC pipe, or whatever you come across at the hardware store that seems to fit the bill.

A bit of experimentation is called for here. If the project is very tall or top heavy you will probably need to stabilize the base somewhat with extra weight; wooden blocks or beanbag weights work well. Remember, you will be adding significantly to the weight by the addition of fabrics and batting. Once it's finished it's hard to go back inside to add stabilizers.

When you have completed the armature, you can use batting to cover it, wrapping and tucking and perhaps taking a stitch or two with upholstery thread and a soft sculpture needle. Build up the batting layer by layer to create a smooth surface.

To create the outer "skin," simply drape the fabrics over the armature and pin in place to fit. Mark all seams with air soluble markers or a chalk marker. Remove fabrics and stitch together being sure to leave openings so that you can slip the finished outer cover over the armature. Certain techniques such as wrapping lend themselves to this method. You can combine the pattern making methods as necessary in order to meet the particular needs of your project.

Designing your own projects from start to finish is a process of trial and error in which serendipity is a major ingredient. Your willingness to experiment will reward you with tremendous creative satisfaction.

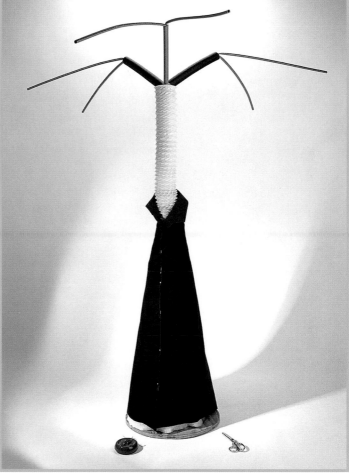

139

Soft Sculpture Resource Guide

Listed are names and addresses of manufacturers and suppliers of many of the products used in this book.

1. Fairfield Processing, Inc.
88 Rose Hill Avenue
Danbury CT 06813
Batting, stuffing and polyester pellets

2. Handler Textile Corp.
24 Empire Boulevard
Moonachie, NJ 07074
Fusible tricot, perforated embroidery stabilizer

3. Thermoweb
770 Glenn Avenue
Wheeling, IL 60090
Fusible web

4. Kreinik Manufacturing Co., Inc.
3106 Timanus Lane, Suite 101
Baltimore, MD 21244
Decorative metallic threads and cords

5. Madeira Marketing, Ltd.
600 East 9th Street
Michigan City, IN 46360
Rayon embroidery threads, trims

6. C. W. Fifield Co., Inc.
4 Keith Way
Hingham, MA 02043
Simulated suede fabrics

7. Farris Enterprises, Inc.
629 Cherokee Avenue
Atlanta, GA 30312
Foam-backed nylon fleece fabric

8. Velcro USA, Inc.
406 Brown Avenue
Manchester, NH 03108
Hook and loop fasteners

Pattern Section

Metric Equivalents
Inches to Millimetres and Centimetres
MM – millimetres   CM – centimetres

Inches	MM	CM	Inches	CM	Inches	CM
1/8	3	0.3	9	22.9	30	76.2
1/4	6	0.6	10	25.4	31	78.7
3/8	10	1.0	11	27.9	32	81.3
1/2	13	1.3	12	30.5	33	83.8
5/8	16	1.6	13	33.0	34	86.4
3/4	19	1.9	14	35.6	35	88.9
7/8	22	2.2	15	38.1	36	91.4
1	25	2.5	16	40.6	37	94.0
1 1/4	32	3.2	17	43.2	38	96.5
1 1/2	38	3.8	18	45.7	39	99.1
1 3/4	44	4.4	19	48.3	40	101.6
2	51	5.1	20	50.8	41	104.1
2 1/2	64	6.4	21	53.3	42	106.7
3	76	7.6	22	55.9	43	109.2
3 1/2	89	8.9	23	58.4	44	111.8
4	102	10.2	24	61.0	45	114.3
4 1/2	114	11.4	25	63.5	46	116.8
5	127	12.7	26	66.0	47	119.4
6	152	15.2	27	68.6	48	121.9
7	178	17.8	28	71.1	49	124.5
8	203	20.3	29	73.7	50	127.0

Metric Conversion Chart					
Yards	Inches	Metres	Yards	Inches	Metres
1/8	4.5	0.11	1 1/8	40.5	1.03
1/4	9	0.23	1 1/4	45	1.14
3/8	13.5	0.34	1 3/8	49.5	1.26
1/2	18	0.46	1 1/2	54	1.37
5/8	22.5	0.57	1 5/8	58.5	1.49
3/4	27	0.69	1 3/4	63	1.60
7/8	31.5	0.80	1 7/8	67.5	1.71
1	36	0.91	2	72	1.83

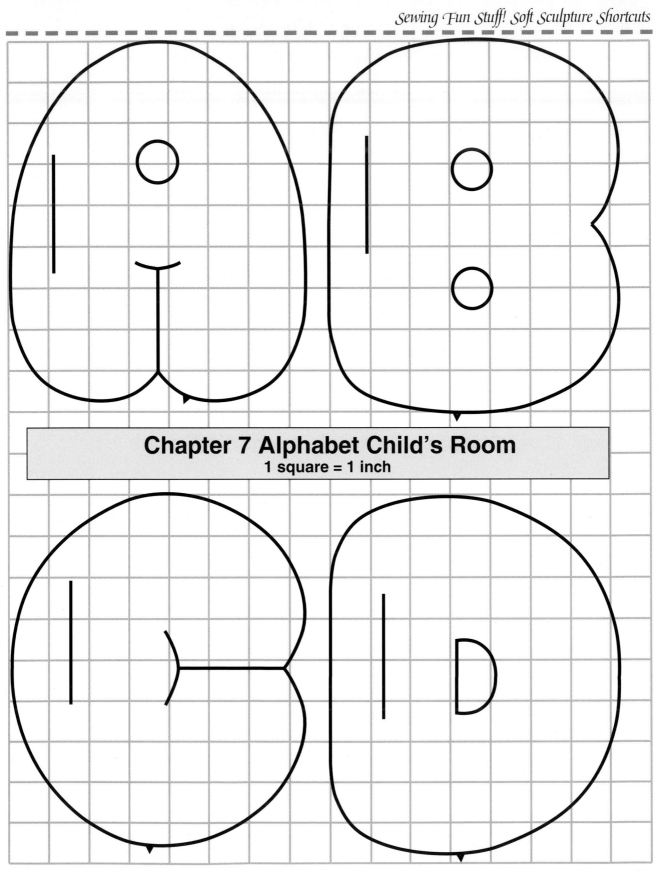

Chapter 7 Alphabet Child's Room
1 square = 1 inch

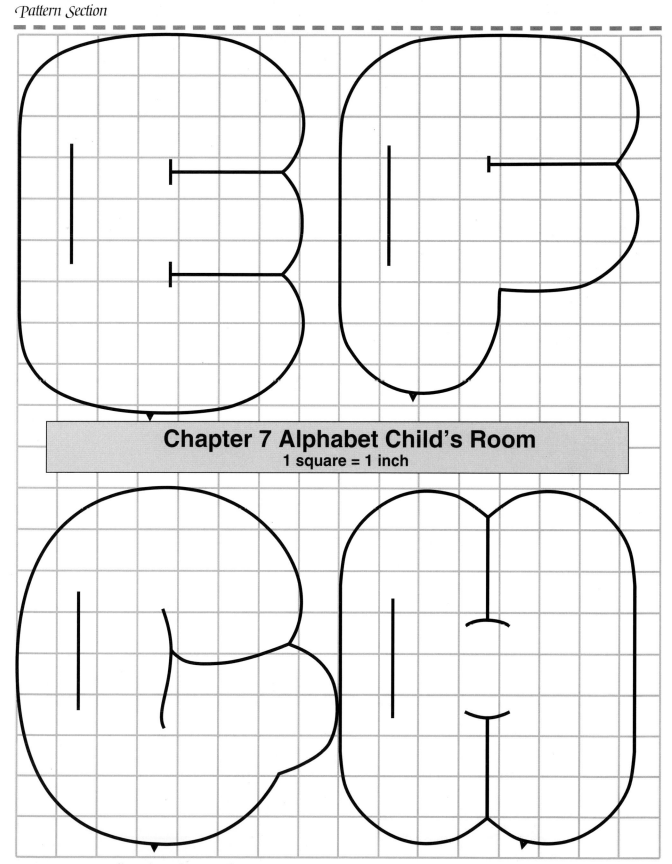

Chapter 7 Alphabet Child's Room
1 square = 1 inch

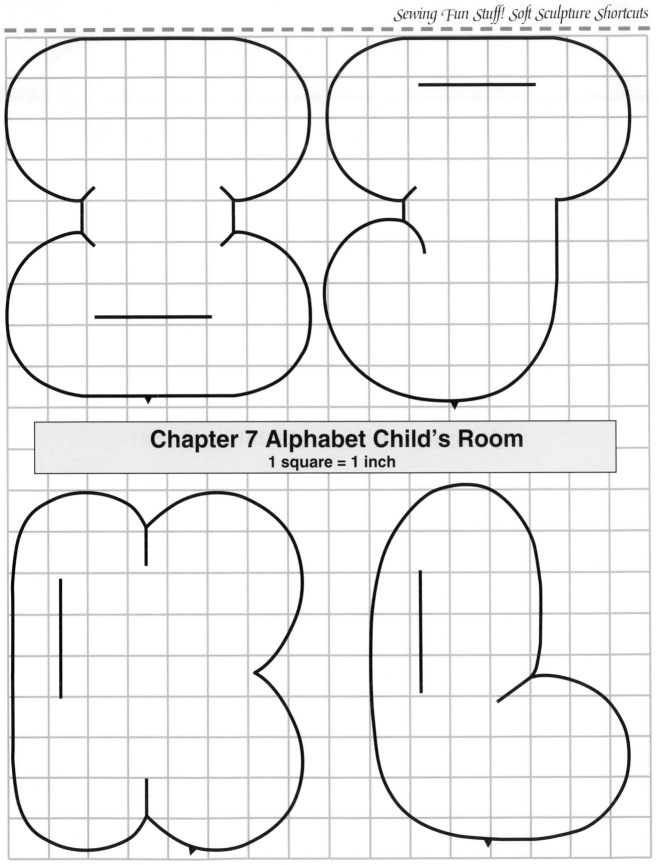

Chapter 7 Alphabet Child's Room
1 square = 1 inch

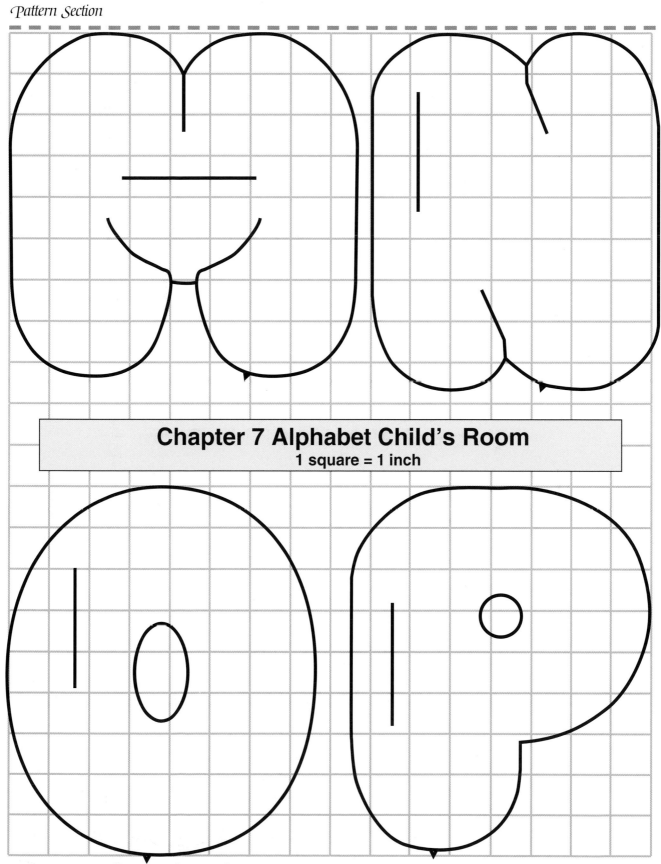

Chapter 7 Alphabet Child's Room
1 square = 1 inch

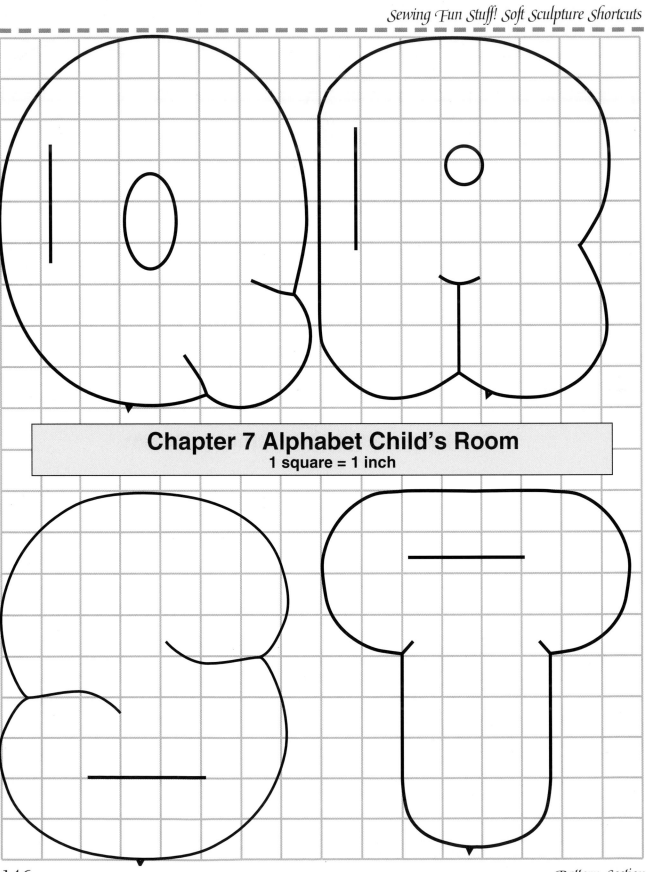

Chapter 7 Alphabet Child's Room
1 square = 1 inch

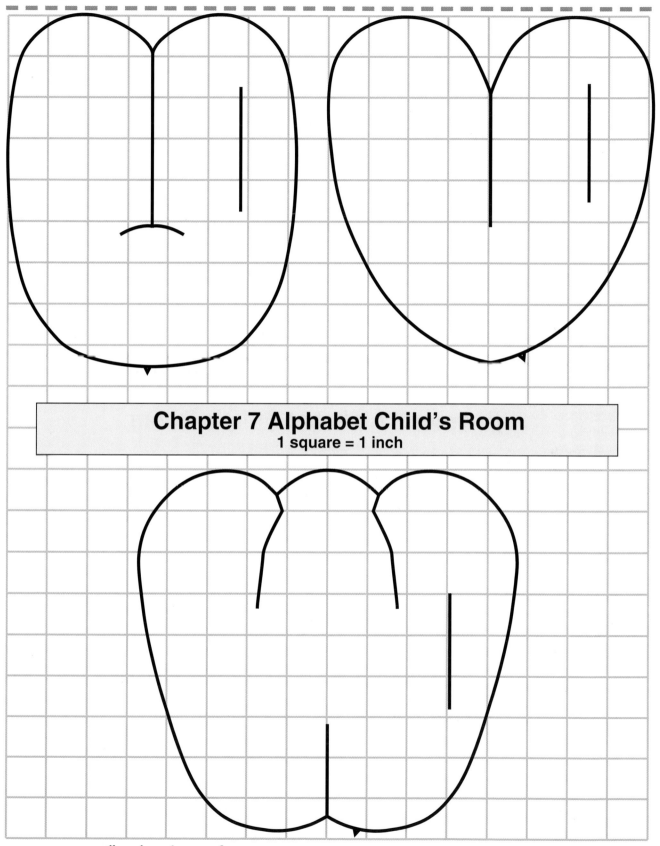

Chapter 7 Alphabet Child's Room
1 square = 1 inch

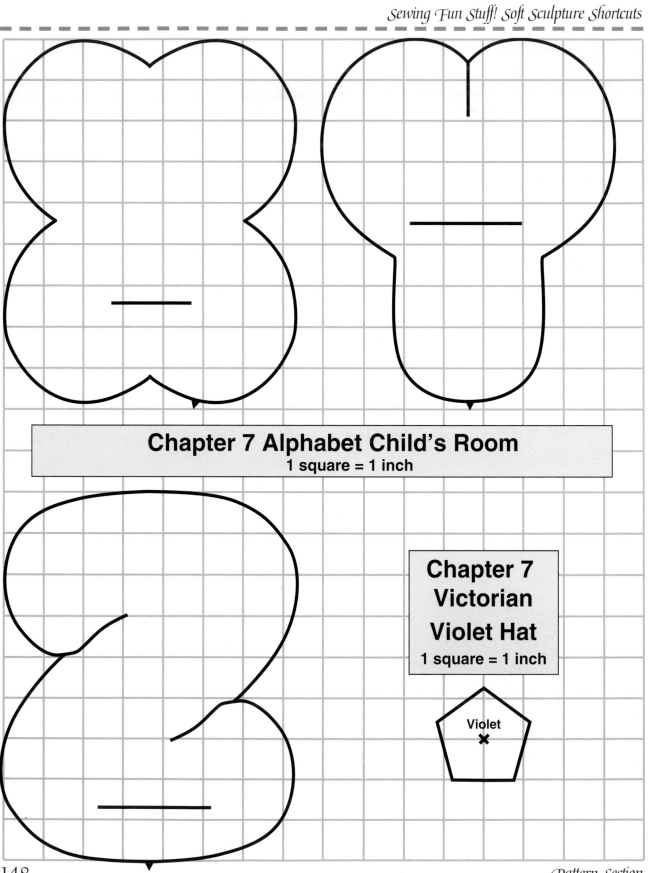

Chapter 7 Alphabet Child's Room
1 square = 1 inch

**Chapter 7
Victorian
Violet Hat**
1 square = 1 inch

Violet
✕

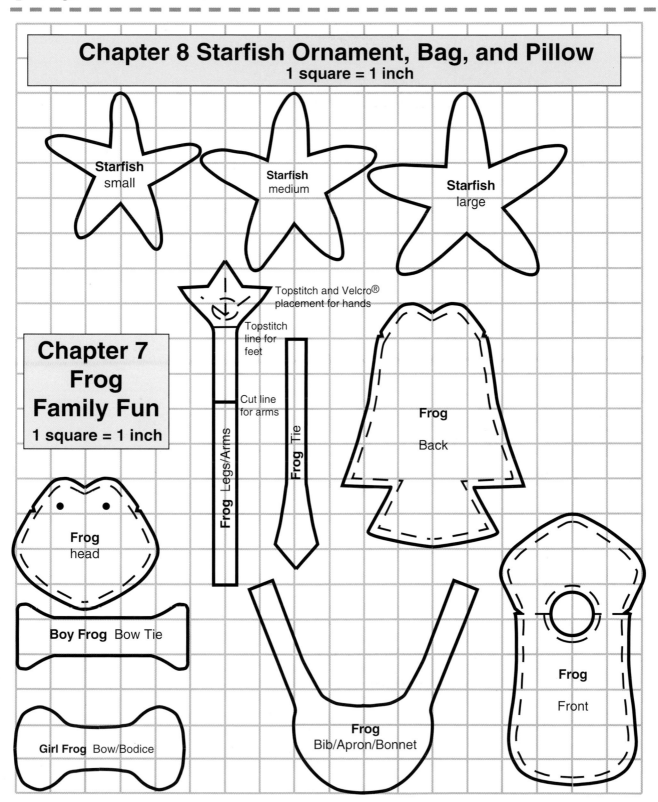

Chapter 8 Starfish Ornament, Bag, and Pillow
1 square = 1 inch

Starfish
small

Starfish
medium

Starfish
large

Topstitch and Velcro®
placement for hands

Topstitch
line for
feet

Cut line
for arms

Frog Legs/Arms

Frog Tie

Frog
Back

Chapter 7
Frog
Family Fun
1 square = 1 inch

Frog
head

Boy Frog Bow Tie

Girl Frog Bow/Bodice

Frog
Bib/Apron/Bonnet

Frog

Front

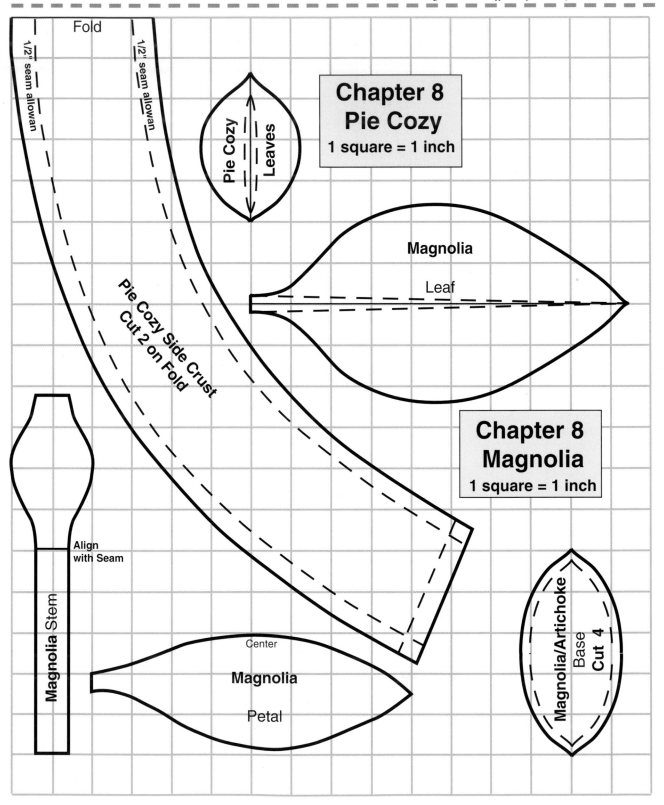

Fold

1/2" seam allowan

1/2" seam allowan

Pie Cozy Leaves

**Chapter 8
Pie Cozy**
1 square = 1 inch

Pie Cozy Side Crust
Cut 2 on Fold

Magnolia

Leaf

**Chapter 8
Magnolia**
1 square = 1 inch

Align with Seam

Magnolia Stem

Center

Magnolia

Petal

Magnolia/Artichoke
Base
Cut 4

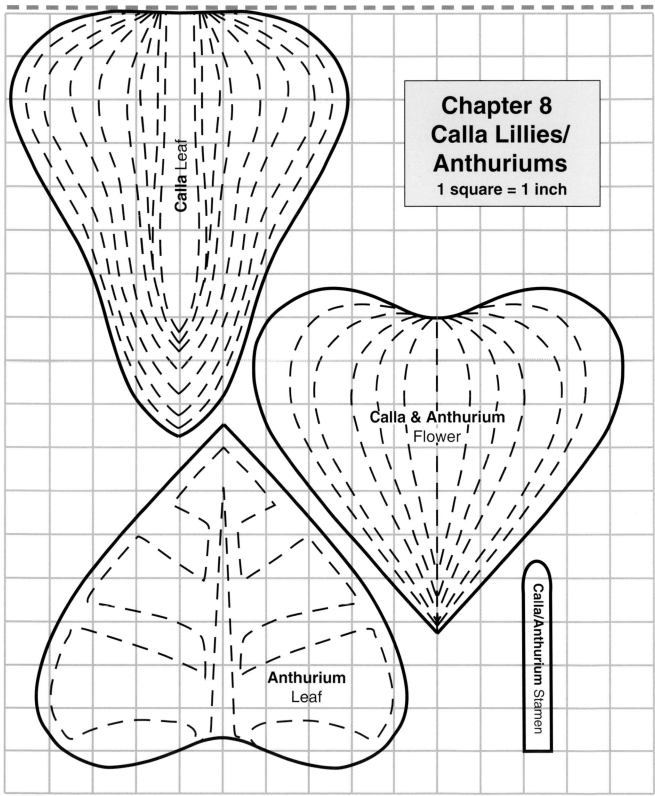

**Chapter 8
Calla Lillies/
Anthuriums**
1 square = 1 inch

Calla Leaf

Calla & Anthurium
Flower

Anthurium
Leaf

Calla/Anthurium Stamen

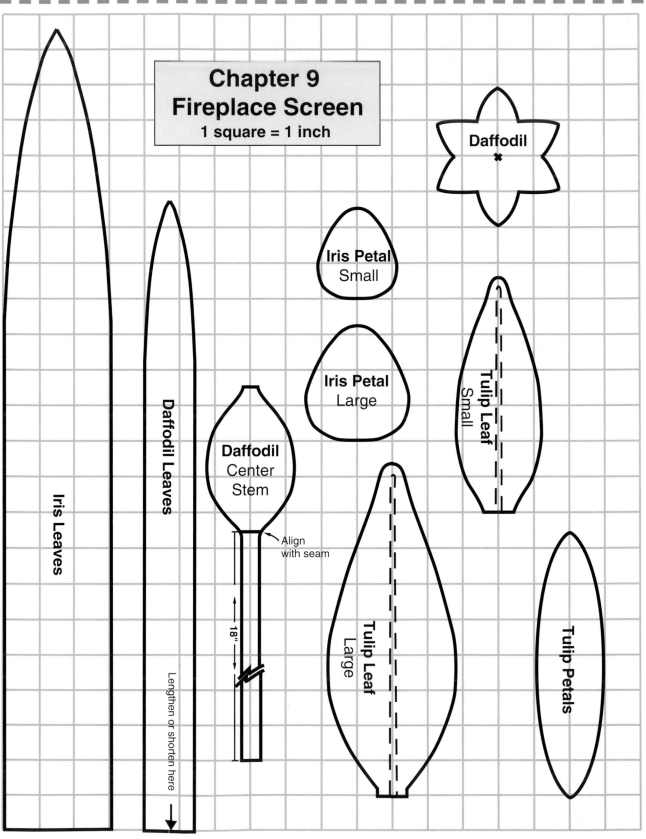

**Chapter 9
Fireplace Screen**

1 square = 1 inch

Daffodil

Iris Petal
Small

Iris Petal
Large

Daffodil
Center
Stem

Align
with seam

18"

Iris Leaves

Daffodil Leaves

Lengthen or shorten here

Tulip Leaf
Small

Tulip Leaf
Large

Tulip Petals

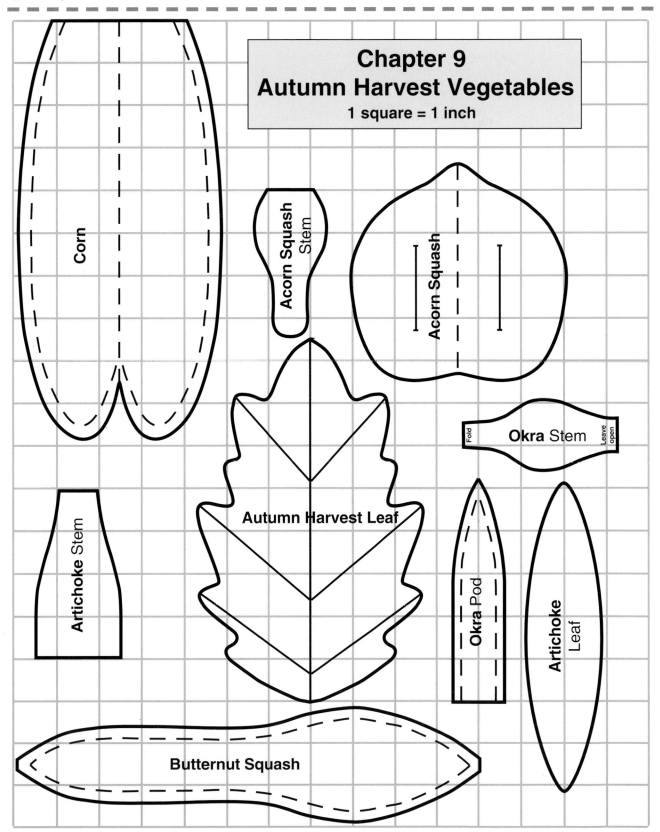

**Chapter 9
Autumn Harvest Vegetables**
1 square = 1 inch

Corn

Acorn Squash Stem

Acorn Squash

Okra Stem

Fold

Leave open

Artichoke Stem

Autumn Harvest Leaf

Okra Pod

Artichoke Leaf

Butternut Squash

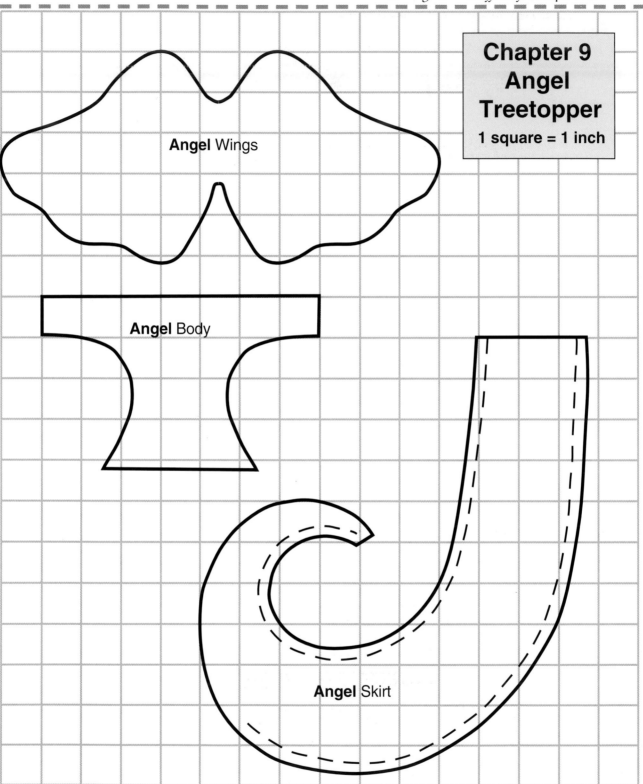

**Chapter 9
Angel
Treetopper**
1 square = 1 inch

Angel Wings

Angel Body

Angel Skirt

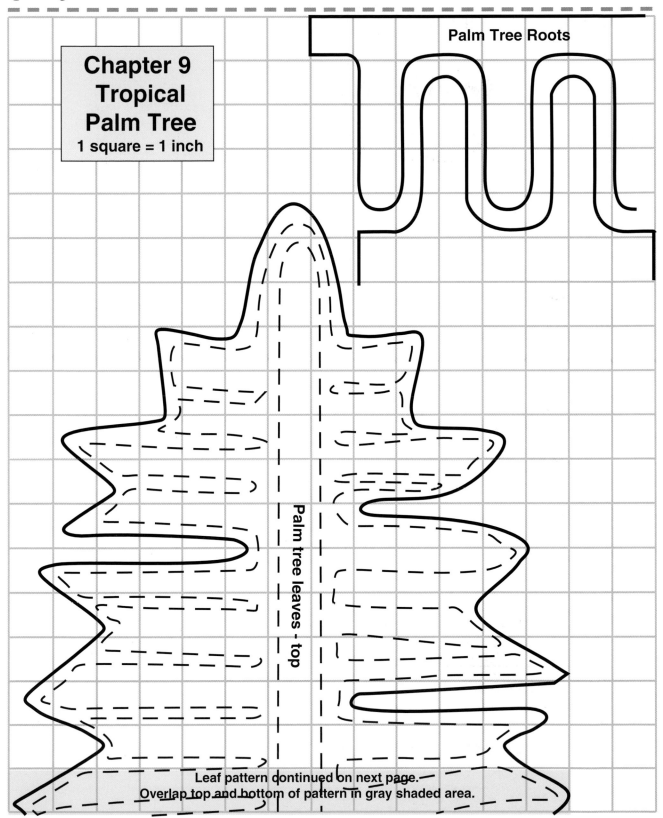

Palm Tree Roots

Chapter 9
Tropical
Palm Tree
1 square = 1 inch

Palm tree leaves - top

Leaf pattern continued on next page.
Overlap top and bottom of pattern in gray shaded area.

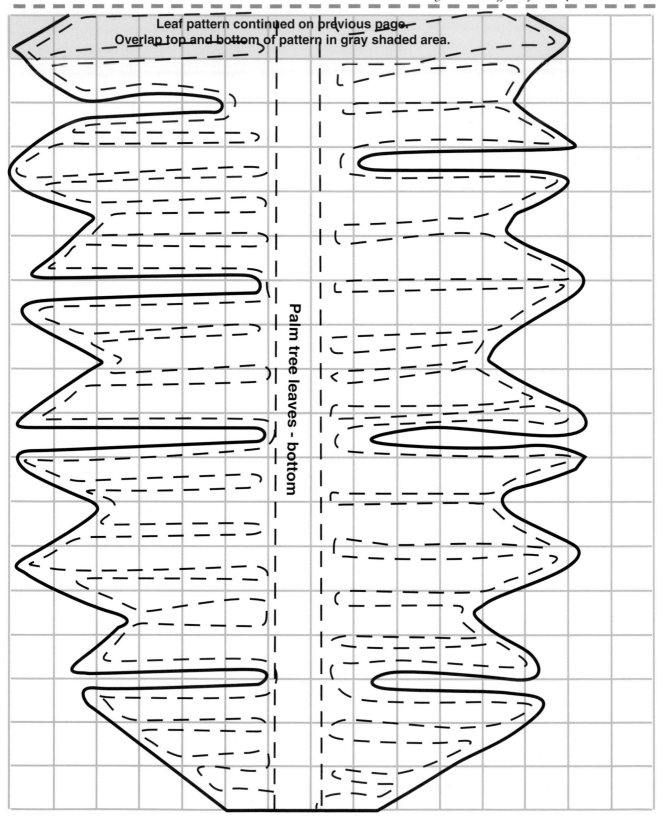

Leaf pattern continued on previous page.
Overlap top and bottom of pattern in gray shaded area.

Palm tree leaves - bottom

Lynne Farris
Big Ideas with a Soft Touch™

Award winning, nationally recognized designer, Lynne Farris brings years of experience in the medium of soft sculpture to the world of crafting.

Trained as a visual artist, she earned a MFA degree before beginning her career as an art instructor, then worked for several years in product development in the toy and juvenile products industries.

In 1982 Lynne founded Farris Enterprises, Inc., a creative service company specializing in the design and creation of promotional characters, properties for licensing and entertainment services. Some of her clients include the Atlanta Hawks, the Atlanta Braves, TBS, Bank South, Herculon, Inc., Bernina of America, The Georgia Renaissance Festival, Egleston Children's Hospital at Emory University, and Georgia's Department of Industry, Trade, and Tourism.

Lynne's whimsical soft sculpture designs are often featured in leading consumer magazines including *Sewing Decor, Crafts, McCall's Quilting,* Better Homes and Gardens Special Interest Publications and Bernina's *Creative Sewing* magazine, and in books by Oxmoor House and Rodale Press. She has designed patterns for *McCall's Creates* and Simplicity Pattern Company. She appears frequently on nationally televised craft programs on the Learning Channel and the Discovery Channel and has taught at national sewing seminars and trade shows, demonstrating her unique soft sculpture techniques.

She is a Certified Craft Designer and is currently serving on the board of directors of SCD. She was the recipient of the 1992 Loctite SCD Scholarship through which she attended Penland School of Crafts in North Carolina to study Japanese textiles. She was recently selected as one of five finalists for the 1994 Craft Designer of the Year Award.

To every challenge Lynne brings a fresh approach and limitless creative energy.

157

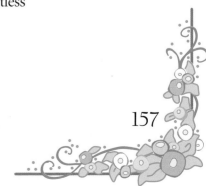

Index

A

acorn squash (advanced project), 100–101
advanced projects
    angel treetopper, 112–117
    fireplace screen, 104–111
    palm tree, 118–125
    vegetables, 94–103
    See also beginner projects; intermediate projects
alphabet child's room (beginner project), 52–53
angel treetopper (advanced project), 112–117
anthuriums (intermediate project), 80–85
armatures (support structures), 22, 138–139
artichoke (advanced project), 99–100

B

batting, 22, 42
    resource guide, 140
beads, 49
beginner projects
    alphabet child's room, 52–53
    cactus everlasting, 54–57
    frog family, 58–63
    hat with violets, 64–65
    See also advanced projects; intermediate projects
berry pie cozy, 68–71
bias cuts, 19
braiding foot, 6, 31, 46
braids, 46
butternut squash (advanced project), 98
buttons, 49

C

cactus everlasting (beginner project), 54–57
calla lillies (intermediate project), 80–85
chalk wheels/wedges, 21
child's room, 20, 52–53
circular embroidery attachments, 30, 38
colors, 18–19, 131–132
cording foot, 31
cords, 46
corn (advanced project), 95–97
curved seams, trimming and turning, 41

D

daffodils (advanced project), 105–107
dolls, 13
draping, 34

E

embellishments, 25
embroidery
    circular attachments for, 30
    decorative with machine, 47
evening bag with starfish ornament (intermediate project), 72–79

F

fabric content, 20
fabrics
    faille, 72
    fleece, 52, 54, 58, 68, 118
    fusing, 35
    organza, 72
    satin or moire, 64, 72, 80, 104, 112
    sources, 18, 140
    suedecloth, 86, 94
    velvet/velour, 72, 80, 118
features advantageous to creating soft sculpture, 27–29
feet, 30-31
fiberfill, 42
finishing touches, 45–49
fireplace screen (advanced project), 104–111
flowers
    calla lillies and anthuriums, 80–85
    daffodils, 105–107
    iris, 109–110
    and leaves, 102–103
    magnolias, 86–91
    tulips, 108
    violets (on hat), 64–65
foot (presser)
    for braiding, 31, 46

form/space, 129–130
frog family (beginner project), 58–63
funnels, 42
fusibles, 21–22
   resource guide, 140
fusing fabrics, 35, 43

G

gathering, 40
gimp (trims), 25, 46
glue guns, 24, 42
gluing, 43
grain of fabric, 19

H

hammers, 24
hand stitching, 49
harvest vegetables (advanced project), 94-103
hat with violets (beginner project), 64–65

I

inspiration sources, 132–135
interfacings, 21–22
intermediate projects
   all-American pie cozy, 68–71
   calla lillies and anthuriums, 80–85
   magnolias, 86–91
   starfish ornament, evening bag or pillow, 72–79
   See also advanced projects; beginner projects
iris (advanced project), 109–110
ironing/pressing, 42
iron-on transfer pens, 21

K

kalaga (Thai wall hanging), 10–11, 12

L

leaves (advanced project), 102–103
line, 128
linear quilting, 39

M

machine embroidery, 47
machines. *See* sewing machines
magnolias (intermediate project), 86–91

map measures, 24
markers, 21
measuring devices, 24
models of soft sculpture project ideas, 135–138

N

needle-nose pliers, 24
needles
   for beading, 49
   importance of using appropriate size, 28
   positioning up-down, 28
   for topstitching, 47

O

okra (advanced project), 97

P

packing peanuts, 22
paintbrushes, 24
palm tree (advanced project), 118–125
pattern in fabric, 19
patterns
   advantages of using, 33
   pre-assembling of contrasting colors, 35
   seam allowances, 35
   transferring onto fabric, 34
pens, 21
pie cozy (intermediate project), 68–71
pillow with starfish ornament (intermediate project), 72–79
pleating, 40
pliers, 24
polyester fiberfill, 42
polyester pellets, 22, 42
pre-programmed stitches, 29
pressing, 42
project design
   armatures/support, 138–139
   construction considerations, 134–135
   envisioning, 128–132
   finding inspiration, 132–133
   modeling in paper, 135–138
projects. *See* advanced projects; beginner projects; intermediate projects

Q

quilting, 39
quiltmaking, 15

R

ribbons, wire-edged, 48

S

saws, 24
screwdrivers, 24
seam allowances, 35
sergers, 15
    for wire-edged ribbons, 48
sewing machines, 15
    features useful for soft sculpture, 27–29
shape, 129
shortcuts for sewing, 37–43
soft sculpture
    origins, 11–15
    project design, 127–139
    resource guide, 140
    See also advanced projects; beginner projects;
        intermediate projects
squash (advanced project), 98, 100–101
stabilizers, 19
starfish ornament, evening bag or pillow
        (intermediate project), 72–79
stitches
    basting/long, 29
    with circular embroidery attachment, 30, 38, 47
    pre-programmed, 29
stitching
    by hand, 49
    flat joining seams, 40
    gathering, 40
    pleating, 40
    prior to cutting, 39
    quilting, 39
    stacks of fabric, 38
    topstitching, 39
    tucking, 40
stones as decoration, 49
straws, 42
stretchability of fabric, 19

stuffings, 22
    resource guide, 140
stuffing sewn objects, 41–42
stuffing tools, 24
styrofoam peanuts, 22
supply resources, 140
support structures (armatures), 22, 138–139

T

tassels, 46
tension adjustment on thread, 28
textures, 19, 130–131
    with topstitching, 47
Thai wall hanging (illustration), 10–11, 12
thread, 20–21
    resource guide, 140
    tension adjustment, 28
tools, 24
topstitching, 39, 47
trapunto, 47
trims, 25, 46
    resource guide, 140
trinkets as decoration, 49
tucking, 40
tulips (advanced project), 108
turning curves, 41
    slashing two-layer shapes, 41

U

upholstery, 14

V

value of light, 130
vegetables (advanced project), 94–103
Victorian violet hat (beginner project), 64–65

W

wall hanging (illustration), 10–11, 12
weight of fabric, 19
wire cutters, 24
wire-edged ribbons, 48
wrapping, 48